A guide to the English tongue. In two parts. ... By the late Rev. Thomas Dyche. A new edition, corrected and enlarged.

Thomas Dyche

ECCO
PRINT EDITIONS

A guide to the English tongue. In two parts. ... By the late Rev. Thomas Dyche. A new edition, corrected and enlarged.
Dyche, Thomas
ESTCID: T113324
Reproduction from British Library

London : printed only for W. Bent, 1796.
[8],160p.,plates : ill.,port. ; 12°

Gale ECCO Print Editions

Relive history with *Eighteenth Century Collections Online*, now available in print for the independent historian and collector. This series includes the most significant English-language and foreign-language works printed in Great Britain during the eighteenth century, and is organized in seven different subject areas including literature and language; medicine, science, and technology; and religion and philosophy. The collection also includes thousands of important works from the Americas.

The eighteenth century has been called "The Age of Enlightenment." It was a period of rapid advance in print culture and publishing, in world exploration, and in the rapid growth of science and technology – all of which had a profound impact on the political and cultural landscape. At the end of the century the American Revolution, French Revolution and Industrial Revolution, perhaps three of the most significant events in modern history, set in motion developments that eventually dominated world political, economic, and social life.

In a groundbreaking effort, Gale initiated a revolution of its own: digitization of epic proportions to preserve these invaluable works in the largest online archive of its kind. Contributions from major world libraries constitute over 175,000 original printed works. Scanned images of the actual pages, rather than transcriptions, recreate the works *as they first appeared.*

Now for the first time, these high-quality digital scans of original works are available via print-on-demand, making them readily accessible to libraries, students, independent scholars, and readers of all ages.

For our initial release we have created seven robust collections to form one the world's most comprehensive catalogs of 18th century works.

Initial Gale ECCO Print Editions collections include:

History and Geography

Rich in titles on English life and social history, this collection spans the world as it was known to eighteenth-century historians and explorers. Titles include a wealth of travel accounts and diaries, histories of nations from throughout the world, and maps and charts of a world that was still being discovered. Students of the War of American Independence will find fascinating accounts from the British side of conflict.

Social Science

Delve into what it was like to live during the eighteenth century by reading the first-hand accounts of everyday people, including city dwellers and farmers, businessmen and bankers, artisans and merchants, artists and their patrons, politicians and their constituents. Original texts make the American, French, and Industrial revolutions vividly contemporary.

Medicine, Science and Technology

Medical theory and practice of the 1700s developed rapidly, as is evidenced by the extensive collection, which includes descriptions of diseases, their conditions, and treatments. Books on science and technology, agriculture, military technology, natural philosophy, even cookbooks, are all contained here.

Literature and Language

Western literary study flows out of eighteenth-century works by Alexander Pope, Daniel Defoe, Henry Fielding, Frances Burney, Denis Diderot, Johann Gottfried Herder, Johann Wolfgang von Goethe, and others. Experience the birth of the modern novel, or compare the development of language using dictionaries and grammar discourses.

Religion and Philosophy

The Age of Enlightenment profoundly enriched religious and philosophical understanding and continues to influence present-day thinking. Works collected here include masterpieces by David Hume, Immanuel Kant, and Jean-Jacques Rousseau, as well as religious sermons and moral debates on the issues of the day, such as the slave trade. The Age of Reason saw conflict between Protestantism and Catholicism transformed into one between faith and logic -- a debate that continues in the twenty-first century.

Law and Reference

This collection reveals the history of English common law and Empire law in a vastly changing world of British expansion. Dominating the legal field is the *Commentaries of the Law of England* by Sir William Blackstone, which first appeared in 1765. Reference works such as almanacs and catalogues continue to educate us by revealing the day-to-day workings of society.

Fine Arts

The eighteenth-century fascination with Greek and Roman antiquity followed the systematic excavation of the ruins at Pompeii and Herculaneum in southern Italy; and after 1750 a neoclassical style dominated all artistic fields. The titles here trace developments in mostly English-language works on painting, sculpture, architecture, music, theater, and other disciplines. Instructional works on musical instruments, catalogs of art objects, comic operas, and more are also included.

The BiblioLife Network

This project was made possible in part by the BiblioLife Network (BLN), a project aimed at addressing some of the huge challenges facing book preservationists around the world. The BLN includes libraries, library networks, archives, subject matter experts, online communities and library service providers. We believe every book ever published should be available as a high-quality print reproduction; printed on-demand anywhere in the world. This insures the ongoing accessibility of the content and helps generate sustainable revenue for the libraries and organizations that work to preserve these important materials.

The following book is in the "public domain" and represents an authentic reproduction of the text as printed by the original publisher. While we have attempted to accurately maintain the integrity of the original work, there are sometimes problems with the original work or the micro-film from which the books were digitized. This can result in minor errors in reproduction. Possible imperfections include missing and blurred pages, poor pictures, markings and other reproduction issues beyond our control. Because this work is culturally important, we have made it available as part of our commitment to protecting, preserving, and promoting the world's literature.

GUIDE TO FOLD-OUTS MAPS and OVERSIZED IMAGES

The book you are reading was digitized from microfilm captured over the past thirty to forty years. Years after the creation of the original microfilm, the book was converted to digital files and made available in an online database.

In an online database, page images do not need to conform to the size restrictions found in a printed book. When converting these images back into a printed bound book, the page sizes are standardized in ways that maintain the detail of the original. For large images, such as fold-out maps, the original page image is split into two or more pages

Guidelines used to determine how to split the page image follows:

• Some images are split vertically; large images require vertical and horizontal splits.
• For horizontal splits, the content is split left to right.
• For vertical splits, the content is split from top to bottom.
• For both vertical and horizontal splits, the image is processed from top left to bottom right.

Rev. *Thomas Dyche*.

A
GUIDE
TO THE
𝕰𝖓𝖌𝖑𝖎𝖘𝖍 𝕿𝖔𝖓𝖌𝖚𝖊.
IN TWO PARTS.

The *First*, proper for *Beginners*, shewing a *Natural* and *Easy* Method to pronounce and express both *Common* Words, and *Proper* Names, in which particular Care is had to shew the *Accent*, for preventing *Vicious Pronunciation*.

The *Second*, for such as are advanced to some *Ripeness* of *Judgment*, containing Observations on the *Sounds* of *Letters* and *Diphthongs*; Rules for the true *Division* of *Syllables*, and the Use of *Capitals*, *Stops*, and *Marks*. With large Tables of *Abbreviations*, and *Distinctions* of Words, and several *Alphabets* of *Copies* for Young Writers.

To which is added

An APPENDIX, containing many additional Lessons, in Prose and Verse, *First*, in Words of One Syllable only; and then mixed with Words of Two, Three, Four, Five, Six, and Seven Syllables. And further improved with new F A B L E S and C U T S.

By the late Rev. THOMAS DYCHE.

A NEW EDITION, corrected and enlarged.

LONDON:
Printed *only* for W. BENT, Pater-noster Row.
MDCCXCVI.

TO THE

Worthy MEMBERS and PROMOTERS of the SOCIETY, united for the CLOATHING and TUITION of an HUNDRED POOR BOYS, in the Parish of St. Giles, Cripplegate.

GENTLEMEN,

YOU were pleased kindly to receive the *former Edition* of this *Guide* to our *Mother-Tongue*, which encourages me to hope, that it may be still more acceptable to you with *Additions* and *Improvements*, and that not only the *Children* of your own *Charity School*, but many others also, may reap the *Benefit* designed for them, both in the *Compiling* and *Publishing* of it.

I cannot but, with the greatest *Joy* and *Sincerity*, congratulate the *wonderful Success* you have lately had in the unanimous Promotion of your truly noble *Design*. The generous Legacy of 200l. left you by Mr *Thomas More*, wherewith you were enabled to purchase a Piece of *Ground*, the plentiful *Contributions* you have procured for *Erecting* the Charity *School* and *Dwelling-house* for the *Master* and *Mistress*; with that *extraordinary Addition* of 1500l. from The Honourable the *Lady Eleanor Hollis*, for the *Endowment* of your *Girls School*, are manifest *Declarations*, that you have the *Finger of God* co-operating with you in that good and charitable Undertaking.

Go on still, *Gentlemen*, with your *wonted Alacrity*, and may your *unwearied Zeal* and *Industry* be (as they justly deserve) a standing *Pattern*, not only to be *admired*, but *imitated*, by all *Christendom*.

I have no more to add, but that I beg the *Favour* to be esteemed,

GENTLEMEN,

Your Humble Servant, and Well-wisher,

From Dean-Street, in Fetter-Lane, Oct, 27, 1709.

Tho. Dyche.

A 2

THE

PREFACE.

ERRORS *in the first Principles are of the most dangerous Consequence. And as this Maxim is most evidently true in Religion, Science, and even in every Mechanic Profession. so also we find, it has its proper Weight in the Study of Languages, and particularly in our own, which is too frequently deprav'd from the very first Foundation, by vicious Pronunciation, ill Spelling, and worse Writing. Children are wrong taught at their first setting out, and neglected in their Progress, so that their Errors grow up with them; and that which would have been their greatest Accomplishment, viz the proper speaking and writing of their Mother-Tongue, is either wholly despised, or at least despaired of, as a Thing altogether unattainable.*

In order to remedy, or rather to prevent, these pittable Inconveniencies, the following Work has appeared several Times abroad in the World; and if we may judge by the kind Acceptance it has found, there is great Hope, that the Reformation is not only begun in the English Tongue, but has by this Time made some considerable Progress, since not only in the Charity Schools, but in many other private Schools, this has been made use of to teach Children from their very Letters. And I do know, that, by a right Use only of this Book, a Child may be brought to read any Chapter in the Bible, or any other Piece of Modern English.

The Monofyllables make up a very considerable Part of our Language; and though I am sensible I have not set down all, yet

The PREFACE.

I am sure, I have far the greatest Part And if these be taught without Book, as well as within, the Teacher will find a great Advantage in it, because, as Words of the same Sound are set jingling together, the Learner will take and apply the Sounds with the greater Ease and Advantage.

When the Tyro is perfect in these, and comes to Words of more Syllables, he will find it to be of great Advantage that the Words are ranked in Tables alphabetically, according to the Bearing of their Accent, for which there is always Direction given in the Beginning of the Chapter, and this is one great Means to prevent Mis-pronunciation And here also, when the Learner can read the Words, I would have him exercised in committing to Memory a certain Quantity every Day, according as his Capacity will bear. And by this Means, in going it twice over, a Person, that has not the Advantage of Skill in the Learned Languages, shall be able to spell readily all, or the most common and difficult Words, that are made use of in the English Tongue.

As to the Dividing of Syllables, the learned Philologers themselves are not agreed in their Opinions · For some would have us stick close to the Latin Rule, laid down in our common Grammars, as thinking it most commendable, that our Language be reduced to the Standard of the Learned Languages. While others are of Opinion with Comenius, " That " Consonants should be join'd with that Vowel that gives " the softest Sound to the Ear.' And I must confess, that in teaching Children to read I think the Ear is the best Guide. But I have found out a Method, which probably will oblige both Parties For the Words are divided according to the Rules of the Latin Grammarians And where a Consonant would sound better to the Ear, with the following Vowel, than that before it, I have placed this Mark (") which was invented purely for this Purpose; and I call it the Double Accent, because the Bearing of the Accent or Stress of the Voice, upon that Syllable, draws the Consonant to the preceding Vowel, in the Sounding of the Words, which by the Rule of Spelling ought to be separated from it Thus we spell ve"stry, vi"sit, ba"nish, but we pronounce ves try, vis it, ban-ish. And they that do not like the Latin Rule of Spelling, may with Ease teach by these Tables according to the Ear, because the Words are every where marked, where the Rule and the Ear disagree.

The PREFACE.

The Second Part *is only of Use to such as are tolerably perfect in the first, and have something of* Capacity *I mean, the Rules are such as cannot be easily instilled into mere* Children, *but may exercise even some* grown Persons, *and without any Reflexion upon their Parts, or Ingenuity. It has been acknowledged to me, that several at Men's Estate have not thought it any Shame to improve themselves by those* Rules, *both as to their* Pronunciation, *and* Writing *And how can this Letter, especially, be performed with any Credit, if Regard be not had to the several Uses of the* Letters, Points, Marks, *Abbreviations, and Distinctions of Words? Of all which you will find here perhaps the largest Tables, that are any where extant.*

You have after all these a Collection of several Alphabets of Words fit for Copies ; *and a Touch of the* Modish Hands *themselves, wherein is shewn the* Order *and* Dependance *of* Letters *one upon another, in such a Manner as they ought to be learned · All which cannot but be of* Use, *as well as* Diversion *to the* Learner.

In the whole Performance *I have had the* Advice *and* Approbation *of several of my* Learned Brethren ; *not being willing to depend intirely upon my own* Judgment *in a Matter of such* Consequence *to the* Public *However, I must say this in my own* Behalf *(and I hope it will not pass for any* Breach *of* Modesty) *that the greatest* Part *of my* Life, *has been spent in studying the best* Methods *I could, to promote the* Public Benefit *in my own* Faculty, *and the* Success *has often been answerable to the* Pleasure *I have taken in the* Work. *And whenever that* Time *shall come, which will incapacitate me for the* Public Service *of my* Native Country, *I verily believe,* Life *itself will be but an uneasy* Burden.

To my Ingenious FRIEND, *the* AUTHOR, *upon this judicious and useful Performance.*

WHat! shall a *Son* of *Learning* condescend
   To *childish* Years his helping Hand to lend?
Stoop to a Task, that *Scholars* think below
Their Sphere? Yet such a Task as we must owe
To *Scholarship*, with nicest *Judgment* join'd,
If we would have it perfect in its Kind.
Shall he thus serve his *Country?* and the *Muse*
The Tribute of her just *Applause* refuse?
Too well she knows the *Service* He has done,
That, *Half's* perform'd in what is well *begun*;
That, from a low Foundation must arise
The *Fabric*, that's design'd to reach the *Skies.*
Yet no old-fashion'd Model here you'll view,
But a Contrivance, *Noble, Neat,* and *New:*
And tho' compil'd with *Ornament* and *Grace,*
Yet *Usefulness* has here the chiefest Place.
These Rules are well design'd to take away
The *Scandel* that upon our Nation lay;
Where *Elegance* a Stranger was, and few
The Beauties of their *Mother-Language* knew.
These Rules must rectify both *Tongue* and *Pen*;
If Youth wou'd speak and write like *learned* Men:
For *Foreign Tongues* can ne'er be rightly known,
Unless we're well acquainted with our *Own.*

           N TATE, *Poet Laureat.*

To the Reverend and Ingenious Mr. THOMAS
DYCHE, on his New Edition of the Guide
to the English Tongue.

WHILST *Numbers* strove in the *Olympic Game*,
    To win the *Prize*, and reach immortal *Fame*,
Th' impartial *Judges* singled out the Man,
Who most expertly *fought*, or fleetest *ran*,
The glorious *Garland* the glad *Victor* crown'd,
And clam'rous *Echoes* did his *Praise* resound.
    So numerous *Writers* of the *learn'd Band*,
Whose well design'd Attempts *Renown* command,
With equal *Merit* long expecting staid,
To gain the *Verdict* of the lovely *Maid*.
But all appearing to *Minerva's* View,
She own'd her *Laurel* did belong to you:
All the *Judicious*, with united *Voice*,
Confirm her *Sentence*, and approve her *Choice*.
How great a *Honour* do we justly owe
To those, from whom each *Art* at first did flow?
Some were extoll'd like *Deities* on Earth,
For giving an inferior *Art* its Birth:
Succeeding *Ages* still revere their Name,
And endless *Time* their *Glory* will proclaim.
This just *Essay* you have perform'd so well,
Records will shew, 'twas *Dyche* first learn'd to *Spell*.
Orthography, tho' fair, still prov'd so coy,
That few durst court her, fewer could enjoy,
In such *confused Labyrinths* she rov'd,
The best *Endeavours* unsuccessful prov'd
But you the long wish'd *guiding Clue* have found,
(A Task too hard for *Learning* less profound)
That, by your skilful and most apt *Address*,
She's now grown *gentle*, easy of *Access*,
By *Method*, tho' concise, so plain and true,
That even *Dullards* must improve by you.
So great's your Merit, your Performance such,
Envy's struck dumb, while Love can't say too much.

      Your Friend and Admirer,

                John Williams.

A Guide to the English *Tongue.*

PART I.

The Alphabet of L E T T E R S

English		Roman		Italian		The Names of the Letters.
a	𝔄	a	A	*a*	*A*	ay
b	𝔅	b	B	*b*	*B*	bee
c	ℭ	c	C	*c*	*C*	ſee
d	𝔇	d	D	*d*	*D*	dee
e	𝔈	e	E	*e*	*E*	e
f	𝔉	f	F	*f*	*F*	eff
g	𝔊	g	G	*g*	*G*	jee
h	ℌ	h	H	*b*	*H*	aytſh
i	ℑ	i	I	*i*	*I*	i
j		j	J,	*j*	*J*	jay
k	𝔎	k	K	*k*	*K*	cay
l	𝔏	l	L	*l*	*L*	ell
m	𝔐	m	M	*m*	*M*	em
n	𝔑	n	N	*n*	*N*	en
o	𝔒	o	O	*o*	*O*	o
p	𝔓	p	P	*p*	*P*	pee
q	𝔔	q	Q	*q*	*Q*	cu
r	𝔎	r	R	*r*	*R*	ar
ſ s	𝔖𝔗	ſ s	S	ſ s	*S*	eſs
t		t	T	*t*	*T*	tee
v		v	V	*v*	*V*	vee
u	𝔘	u	U	*u*	*U*	yu
w	𝔚	w	W	*w*	*W*	double uu
x	𝔛	x	X	*x*	*X*	eks
y	𝔜	y	Y	*y*	*Y*	wi
z	𝔷	z	Z	*z*	*Z*	zed

The VOWELS.

a e i o u, *and* y, *when it follows a Consonant.*

The CONSONANTS.

b c d f g h j k l m n p q r s t v w x y z.

Double LETTERS.

 & fi fi fh fl fl ff ff ft ffi ffi ffl æ œ.

CHAP. I.

Of SYLLABLES.

TABLE I.					TABLE II.				
ba	be	bi	bo	bu	ab	eb	ib	ob	ub
ca	ce	ci	co	cu	ac	ec	ic	oc	uc
da	de	di	do	du	ad	ed	id	od	ud
fa	fe	fi	fo	fu	af	ef	if	of	uf
ga	ge	gi	go	gu	ag	eg	ig	og	ug
ha	he	hi	ho	hu	ah	eh	ih	oh	uh
ja	je	ji	jo	ju	ak	ek	ik	ok	uk
ka	ke	ki	ko	ku	al	el	il	ol	ul
la	le	li	lo	lu	am	em	im	om	um
ma	me	mi	mo	mu	an	en	in	on	un
na	ne	ni	no	nu	ap	ep	ip	op	up
pa	pe	pi	po	pu	ar	er	ir	or	ur
qua	que	qui	quo	qu	as	es	is	os	us
ra	re	ri	ro	ru	at	et	it	ot	ut
fa	fe	fi	o	fu	ax	ex	ix	ox	ux
ta	te	ti	to	tu	az	ez	iz	oz	uz
va	ve	vi	vo	vu	amp	emp	imp	omp	ump
wa	we	wi	wo	wu	ant	ent	int	ont	unt
ya	ye	yi	yo	yu	aft	eft	ift	oft	uft
za	ze	zi	zo	zu	ath	eth	ith	oth	uth

TABLE III.

bla	ble	bli	blo	blu	ſla	ſle	ſli	ſlo	ſlu
bra	bre	bri	bro	bru	ſma	ſme	ſmi	ſmo	ſmu
cha	che	chi	cho	chu	ſna	ſne	ſni	ſno	ſnu
cla	cle	cli	clo	clu	ſpa	ſpe	ſpi	ſpo	ſpu
cra	cre	cri	cro	cru	ſqua	ſque	ſqui	ſquo	ſqu
dra	dre	dri	dro	dru	ſta	ſte	ſti	ſto	ſtu
dwa	dwe	dwi	dwo	dwu	ſwa	ſwe	ſwi	ſwo	ſwu
fla	fle	fli	flo	flu	tha	the	thi	tho	thu
fra	fre	fri	fro	fru	tra	tre	tri	tro	tru
gla	gle	gli	glo	glu	twa	twe	twi	two	twu
gna	gne	gni	gno	gnu	wha	whe	whi	who	whu
gra	gre	gri	gro	gru	wra	wre	wri	wro	wru
kna	kne	kni	kno	knu	phra	phre	phri	phro	phru
pha	phe	phi	pho	phu	ſcra	ſcre	ſcri	ſcro	ſcru
pla	ple	pli	plo	plu	ſhra	ſhre	ſhri	ſhro	ſhru
pra	pre	pri	pro	pru	ſpla	ſple	ſpli	ſplo	ſplu
rha	rhe	rhi	rho	rhu	ſpra	ſpre	ſpri	ſpro	ſpru
ſca	ſce	ſci	ſco	ſcu	ſtra	ſtre	ſtri	ſtro	ſtru
ſha	ſhe	ſhi	ſho	ſhu	thra	thre	thri	thro	thru
ſka	ſke	ſki	ſko	ſku	thwa	thwe	thwi	thwo	thwu

CHAP. II.

Significant Words of One Syllable.

TABLE I.

Of Words ending in a single Conſonant.

BAB cab dab mab nab tab blab crab drab ſcab ſlab ſtab ſwab. Deb web Zeb Bib fib gib nib rib crib drib glib ſquib Bob cob fob gob hob job lob mob gnob rob ſob ſquob throb Bub cub dub nub rub tub blub chub club drub frub grub ſnub ſtub ſcrub ſhrub. Bad did gad had lad mad pad ſad wad brad clad glad

A 6

plad ſhad. Bed fed led Ned red Ted wed bled
bred fled ſhed ſped ſhred thred Bid did hid
kid lid rid chid quid Cod Dod God hod jod
nod pod quod rod ſod tod clod plod ſhod trod.
Bud cud dud mud ſpud ſtud. Bag cag fag gag
bag jag lag nag rag tag wag brag crag drag
gag knag ſhag ſnag ſtag ſwag wrag ſcrag.
Beg keg leg Meg peg dreg Big dig fig gig jig
tig pig rig wig grig prig ſwig trig twig whig
ſprig ſtrig. Bog cog dog fog Gog hog jog log
nog clog ſlog frog prog. Bug dug hug jug lug
mug pug rug tug plug ſhug ſlug ſmug ſnug
drug ſhrug. Dam ham pam ram ſam diam
flam ſham ſwam tram. Gem hem Clem ſtem
them. Dim him rim Tim brim Crim grim
prim ſkim ſlim ſwim trim whim. Tom from
whom. Bum gum hum Lum mum num rum
ſum chum crum dium glum grum plum ſcum
ſtum ſwum ſtrum thrum. Ban can Dan fan
man Nan pan ran tan van wan bran clan plan
ſcan ſpan ſwan than Ben den fen hen men peh
ten wen ſken then when wren. Bin din ſin
gin in kin lin pin ſin tin win chin grin ſhin
ſkin ſpin thin ſcrin. Con Don ſon won yon.
Bun dun fun gun Mun nun pun run ſun tun
ſpun ſtun. Cap gap hap lap map nap pap rap
ſap tap chap clap flap ſlap ſnap ſwap trap wrap
ſcrap ſtrap. Hep nep ſtep Dip gip hip jip lip
nip pip rip ſip tip chip clip drip flip ſhip ſkip
ſlip ſnip trip whip ſcrip ſtrip. Fop hop lop mop
pop ſop top chop crop drop flop knop prop ſhop
ſlop ſtop ſtrop. Cup ſup tup grup Bar car far
jar mar par tar war char Czar ſcar ſpar ſtar.
Her Ker. Fir Sir ſtir. Bur cur Hur pur blur
cur ſlur ſpur. Has was. Hus pus plus thus.

Bat cat fat gat hat mat Nat pat that fat tat vat
Wat brat chat gnat plat prat that what fprat
fquat. Bet fet get jet let met net pet fet wet yet
fret tret whet Bit cit fit hit kit nit pit quit fit
tit wit chit flit grit knit fkit flit fpit twit whit writ
fplit fpit Dot got hot jot lot not pot rot fot
wot blot clot knot plot quot fcot fhot fnot fpot
trot. But cut gut hut nut put glut fcut fhut flut
fmut ftrut. By my py bly Bry buy cry dry fly
fiv ply pry fhy fky fly fpy fty thy try vy why wry.

TABLE II.

Of Words ending with two or more Confonants.

EBb. Back hack jack lack pack quack rack fack
tack black clack crack knack flack fmack
fnack ftack track wrack thwack Beck deck keck
neck peck check fpeck. Dick kick lick nick pick
quick tick fick tick wick brick chick crick prick
fpick thick trick thwick Cock dock hock lock
mock pock rock fock block clock crock flock
frock knock fhock fmock ftock. Buck duck luck
muck ruck fuck tuck chuck cluck pluck ftuck
truck ftruck. Act fact pact tract. Sect. Pict ftrict.
Odd. Gaff quaff raff chaff draff ftaff Tiff cliff
fkiff ftiff twiff whiff. Off cloff fcoff Buff cuff huff
luff muff puff ruff bluff gruff fnuff truff. Aft
haft waft craft fhaft. Left left cleft theft. Gift lift
fift drift fhift fhrit thrift. Oft loft croft Cuft tuft
ftuft. Egg Degg Clegg. High nigh figh Fight
light might night fight tight wight right bright
flight fright knight plight flight wright fpright.
Alb. Elb Bald fcald. Geld held. Gild mild wild
child. Old bold cold fold gold hold mold fold told
fcold. Calf half. Elf pelf fhelf. Wolf Balk
calk talk walk chalk ftalk. Elk belk yelk welk.

Bilk milk silk wilk. Folk. Bulk Fulk gulk
hulk sculk. All ball call gall hall mall pall tall
wall shall small stall scrall thrall   Bell cell dell
ell fell gell hell Nell quell sell tell well yell
kell dwell knell shell smell Snell spell swell.   Ill
bill dill fill gill hill jill kill mill nill pill sill till
will chill drill skill spill squill still swill thill
trill shrill Dóll lóll Móll Nóll dróll; Bóll póll róll
tóll stóll scróll   Bull cull dull full gull hull lull
mull null pull scrull trull.   Balm calm palm
qualm psalm. Aims. Elm helm whelm Film.
Holm Culm Ulm. Aln Caln. Alp scalp. Help
yelp whelp   Filp Fulp gulp gulph.   Alt halt
malt salt shalt   Belt felt gelt melt pelt welt smelt
spelt. Gilt guilt hilt jilt milt wilt quilt spilt stilt.
Bolt colt dolt Holt jolt polt Jamb lamb Kemb
wemb Limb Bomb comb tomb womb. Dumb
rumb plumb thumb. Damn. Limn hymn.
Camp damp lamp ramp vamp champ clamp
cramp stamp swamp Hemp Kemp. Gimp
himp limp pimp shimp. Pomp. Bump dump
jump mump pump rump crump frump plump
stump thump trump. Nymph. And band hand
land rand sand wand Bland brand gland grand
stand strand. End bend fend lend mend rend
send tend vend blend spend. Bind find hind
k'nd mind rind wind blind grind twin'd Bond
fond pond strond. Fund shunn'd stunn'd.
Bang fang gang hang rang sang tang flang
slang twang Bing ding ling ring sing wing
bring cling fling sling sting swing thing wring
spring string. Long song prong thong wrong
strong throng tongue. Bung dung hung rung
ung clung flung slung stung swung wrung
strung. Bank hank lank rank sank tank blank

I

crank drank flank frank plank prank fhank
fhrank flank fpank ftank thank twank. Penk.
Ink link pink fink tink wink blink brink chink
clink drink fhrink ftink flink ftink think twink.
Monk. Funk punk funk flunk drunk trunk ftunk
fhrunk. Hunks monks punks trunks. Ann.
Ant cant pant rant want Zant chant grant plant
quant fcant flant. Bent dert Kent lent pent
rent fent tent vent went fcent fhent fpent Trent.
Dint hint lint mint flint fquint Sprint ftint.
Pint. Font pont wont front. Hunt runt blunt
brunt grunt. Apt capt gapt lapt rapt chapt
clapt flapt fnapt ftrapt fwapt trapt wrapt Kept
wept flept ftept fwept. Dipt hipt ript fipt tipt
chipt clipt dript fhipt fkipt flipt tript whipt
ftript Lopt popt fopt topt chopt cropt dropt
propt fhopt flopt ftopt. Barb garb. Herb verb
Kirk Orb. Curb. Barb caid gard hard lard
ward yard chard mari'd. Herd fherd. Bird
gird third. Cord ford lordt word word. Curd
furr'd blurr'd fpurr'd Dwarf fcarf wharf. Turf
fcurf. Ark bark cark dark lark mark park clark
fhark fpark ftark. Jerk yerk clerk querk. Irk
firk fhirk fmirk Cork fork pork work York
ftork Lurk Turk fnurk. Carl marl fnarl. Bir
girl twirl whirl. Curl furl hurl purl churl fnurl.
Arm barm farm harm warm charm fwarm
Term fperm. Firm Form ftorm. Worm. Barn
yarn. Bern dern fern kern yern ftern. Born corn
horn morn torn worn fcorn fhorn fworn thorn.
Urn burn turn churn fpurn. Carp harp warp
fcarp fharp. Querp. Chirp. Thorp. Bàrs càrs
Màrs pàrs ftàrs. Art cart dart fart hart mart
part tart wart chart quart fmart ftart thwart.
Pert yert. Dirt girt flirt fhirt fkirt fpirt fquirt.

Fôrt pôrt ſpôrt Dŏrt mŏrt ſŏrt tŏrt ſhŏrt. Wort
ſnort Curt hurt blurt Sturt Aſh caſh daſh haſh
laſh maſh paſh raſh ſaſh taſh waſh cluſh craſh
firſh flaſh gnaſh plaſh quaſh ſhaſh ſmaſh ſwaſh
traſh ſplaſh ſquaſh Neſh fleſh freſh thieſh Diſh
fiſh kiſh piſh wiſh Shiſh ſwiſh. Buſh huſh guſh
puſh ruſh tuſh bluſh bruſh cruſh fluſh pluſh
ſnuſh thruſh Aſk baſk caſk laſk maſk taſk flaſk.
Deſk   Fiſk riſk briſk rriſk whiſk. Buſk duſk
huſk muſk ruſk tuſk. Aſp gaſp naſp raſp waſp
claſp graſp. Liſp wiſp criſp. Cuſp. Aſs baſs
laſs maſs paſs braſs claſs glaſs Beſs ceſs gueſs
leſs meſs neſs bleſs cheſs dreſs treſs ſtreſs. Biſs
hiſs kiſs miſs piſs bliſs ſwiſs. Boſs joſs loſs moſs
koſs ſoſs toſs croſs droſs gloſs groſs. Buſs fuſs
Huſs truſs Caſt faſt haſt laſt maſt paſt vaſt waſt
blaſt. Beſt gueſt jeſt leſt neſt peſt reſt teſt veſt.
weſt yeſt zeſt bleſt cheſt creſt dreſt queſt wreſt.
Fiſt liſt miſt piſt wiſt griſt twiſt whiſt wriſt.
Coſt loſt toſt croſt froſt Ghôſt hôſt môſt pôſt.
Duſt guſt juſt luſt muſt ruſt cruſt truſt thruſt.
Bath Gath hath lath math path ſwath wrath.
Beth Heth Seth Pith ſith with Frith ſmith. Gŏth
loth moth broth cloth froth troth wroth. Bôth
dôth quoth ſlôth Balch. Belch Welch ſquelch.
Filch milch pilch Hulch. Hanch lanch blanch
branch granch ſtarch Bench quench tenth
wench drench French ſtench tench wrench.
Pinch winch clinch flinch Bunch Dunch hunch
lunch punch. Tenth Ninth. Arch march parch
ſtarch Perch Birch Porch torch ſcorch.
Lurch church. Corps. Harſh marſh. Birth.
Forth worth Firſt thirſt. Built curſt durſt
Hurſt. Batch catch hatch latch match patch
watch cratch ſmatch ſnatch thatch ſcratch.

Fetch ketch letch vetch sketch wretch stretch.
Itch bitch ditch fitch hitch nitch pitch rich witch
flitch stitch switch twitch which Botch hotch
potch notch scotch Dutch hutch crutch much
such.

TABLE III.

*Words with E Final, lengthening the Sound of the
Syllable.*

Babe Glebe. Jibe bribe tribe. Lobe robe
globe. Cube tube. Ace dace face lace mace
pace race brace chace grace place space trace.
Ice dice lice mice nice rice fice tice vice price
flice spice trice twice thrice. Duce Bruce fluce
truce spruce. Bade cade fade jade lade made
wade blade shade slade spade trade. Bede
Mede glede. Bide guide hide ride side tide
wide chide glide pride slide stride. Ode bode
code mode node rode strode. Jude rude crude
Prude. Safe chafe. Fife life rife wife knife strife.
Age cage gage page rage sage wage stage.
Huge. Ake bake cake lake make rake fake
take wake blake brake drake flake quake shake
flake snake spake stake. Eke reke cheke. Dike
like pike tike spike strike. Coke joke poke yoke
broke choke cloke croke smoke spoke stoke.
Duke Luke puke fluke Ale bale cale dale gale
hale male pale sale tale vale wale scale shale
stale Swale whale. Ile file guile mile pile tile vile
wile smile spile stile while Bole cole dole hole
mole pole sole stole whole strole. Bule mule
pule rule yule. Came dame fame game lame
name fame tame blame Brame crame frame
shame Rheme scheme theme. Lime rime time
chime crime grime prime slime thyme. Come

ſome. Dôme fôme home pôme lôme Rôme
tôme blôme Frôme. Fume plume ſpume.
Bane cane Dane Jane lane mane pane vane
wane crane Grane plane ſwane. Dine fine
kine line mine nine pine fine tine vine wine
brine chine ſhine ſwine thine trine twine whine
ſhrine. one gone done. Bône cône hône nône
tône drône ſhône ſtône thrône. June tune
prune. Toe. Shoe Ape cape gape nape rape
tape crape grape ſcape ſhape ſnape ſcrape. Pipe
ripe wipe gripe ſnipe tripe ſtripe. Cope hope
mope nope pope rope ſope tope grope ſcope
ſlope trope. Are bare care dare fare hare
mare pare rare tare ware blare chare clare
glare ſcare hare Slare ſnare ſpare ſquare ſtare
ſware. Bere here mere pere rere vere were
Frere there where. Ire dire fire hire mire quire
fire tire wire ſhire pire ſquire. Bore core fore
gore lore more pore ſore tore wore yore ſcore
ſhore ſnore ſtore ſwore whore. Ure cure dure
lure pure ſure. Baſe caſe graſe Waſe chaſe
phraſe. Ciſe riſe wiſe guiſe. Doſe hoſe loſe noſe
poſe roſe choſe cloſe gloſe proſe thoſe whoſe.
Uſe muſe cruſe. Ate bate date fate gate hate
Kate late mate pate rate ſate tate plate
prate ſcate ſlate ſtate Bite kite mite quite rite
ſite blite ſmite ſmite ſpite trite white write
thwite. Cote dote mote note quote rote vote
blote ſmote wrote. Lothe clothe. Lute mute
flute ſhute. Cue due hue rue ſue blue clue
flue glue Prue ſpue true Cave gave have
rave ſave wave brave lave crave grave knave
ſhave ſlave ſtave thrave. Dive five hive drive
ſtrive thrive. Cives fives knives lives wives.
Give live five. Côve hôve Jôve rôve wôve

clove drove grove ſtrove throve. Dŏve lŏve glŏve ſhŏve mŏve prŏve. Gaze maze blaze craze glaze graze. Badge fadge madge. Edge hedge ledge ſedge wedge dredge fledge pledge ſledge. Fidge ridge bridge. Dodge Hodge lodge ſtodge. Budge judge drudge grudge ſnudge trudge. Mange range change grange ſtrange. Dinge hinge ſinge tinge cringe fringe ſwinge twinge ſpringe. Plunge ſpunge. Farce ſcarce parſe. Barge large charge. Serge verge. Forge gorge. Purge ſurge ſpurge. Hague plague. Rogue vogue.

T A B L E IV.

Of Monoſyllables conſiſting of Diphthongs.

(ai) Laid maid paid ſtaid ſtraid. Straight. Ail bail fail hail jail mail nail pail quail rail ſail tail vail wail flail frail ſnail trail. Aim maim claim. Cain fain gain lain main pain rain vain wain blain brain chain drain grain plain ſkain ſlain Spain ſtain ſwain train twain ſprain ſtrain Faint paint quaint ſaint taint plaint Air fair hair pair chair ſtair. Bait wait plait ſtrait. Faith ſaith.

(ei) Neigh weigh. Feign reign Seine vein. Feint. Seize Heir their. Eight height weight ſleight ſtreight.

(oi) Voice choice. Void Coif. Oil boil coil foil moil poil quoil ſoil toil broil ſpoil. Coin foin join loin groin. Joint point Hoiſe noiſe poize. Foiſt joiſt moiſt. Coit doit foit.

(au) Daub. Baud laud maud fraud Laugh Waugh. Baught caught taught draught fraught.

Aunt daunt haunt jaunt taunt vaunt flaunt flaunt.
Cauſe pauſe clauſe

(eu) Feud. Rheum.

(ou) Thou Ouch gouch pouch touch vouch
crouch flouch Loud cloud croud Stroud.
Gouge. Couch Gough hough ſough tough
trough. Bough plough flough. Dough through.
Ought bought fought nought ſought brought
drought thought wrought. Foul Joul ſoul.
Noun. Ounce bounce flounce trounce Bound
found hound mound pound round ſound wound
ground Count mount Blount. Our pour ſour
flour ſcour. Four tour your. Gourd. Bourn
mourn. Douſe houſe louſe mouſe ſouſe chouſe.
Spouſe rouze. Out bout gout pout rout clout
doubt flout grout ſcout ſhout ſnout ſpout ſtout
trout ſprout. Louth mouth ſouth. Youth.

(ee) Bee fee lee ſee flee free glee knee thee
tree three. Fleece Greece geeſe. Beech leech
breech creech peech ſcreech. Deed feed heed
need reed ſeed weed bleed breed creed freed
ſpeed ſteed Tweed. Beef reef. Leek meek
peek ſeek week cheek creek gleek Greek ſleek.
Feel heel keel peel reel kneel ſteel wheel. Deem
ſeem teem. Been keen ſeen queen ſcreen ſpleen,
Deep keep peep weep creep ſheep ſleep ſteep
ſweep. Beer deer jeer leer peer ſeer veer cheer
freer queer ſteer. Bees fees lees ſees knees trees
leeſe cheeſe breeze freeze ſneeze ſqueeze wheeze.
Beet feet leet meet Peet fleet gleet greet ſheet
ſleet ſweet ſtreet. Teeth. Beeve reeve ſleeve.

(oo) Good hood wood blood flood ſtood.
Food mood rood brood. Hoof loof woof proof.
Book cook hook look nook rook took brook
crook ſhook ſnook. Cool fool pool tool ſchool

ſtool Wŏol Boom coom doom loom room
bloom broom gloom gróom Boon moon noon,
ſoon ſpoon ſwoon Coop hoop loop poop ſoop
droop ſloop ſtoop troop whoop Boot door moor
poor floor. Gooſe looſe nooſe. Fuot fóot. Bôot
côot hôot môot róot tôot ſhôot. Tooth ſooth
ſoothe ſmoothe. Ooze booze.

(ea) Pea ſea tea yea flea plea. Each beach
Keach Leach peach reach teach bleach breach
preach. Dĕad hĕad lĕad rĕad bread drĕad ſtĕad
trĕad ſprĕad Bĕad lêad mêad rêad flêad
knêad piêad. Deaf leaf ſheaf League Beak
leak peak reak weak bleak break creak freak
ſneak ſpeak ſteak ſcreak ſqueak Beal deal heal
meal neal peal ſeal teal wéal ſqueal ſteal wheal.
Rĕalm. Dĕalt. Hĕalth wĕalth ſtĕalth. Beam
ream ſeam team bream cream dream gleam
ſteam ſcream ſtream Bean dean lean mean
wean yean clean glean quean ſtean. Heap
leap reap cheap. Bĕar pĕar tĕar wĕar ſwĕar.
Dêar fêar êar hêar nêar yêar blêar chêar clêar
flêar ſhêar ſmêar ſnêar ſpêar ſtêar. Search. Earl
pearl. Pĕarſe ſĕarſe. Earn leain. Hĕart. Earth
dearth hearth Eaſe peas ſeas teaze fleas pleas
pleaſe. Ceaſe leaſe peaſe creaſe greaſe. Leaſh.
Brĕaſt. Eaſt bêaſt fêaſt lêaſt. Sweat thrĕat. Bêat
êat hêat mêat pêat ſêat têat blêat chêat grêat
trĕat whĕat. Dĕath brĕath ſhĕath. Brêathe
ſheathe wrêathe.

(oa) Coach loach poach roach broach. Goad
load road toad woad broad. Loaf. Oak roak
ſoak. Coal foal goal loal ſhoal. Foam gloam
roam Joan loan moan roan groan Sloan. Oar
boar hoar roar ſoar ſhore. Boaſt coaſt roaſt toaſt.
Boat coat goat moat float groat ſtoat throat.

(ie) Fief brief chief thief. Piece. Liege. Siege. Shriek. Field yield shield. Fiend friend. Fierce pierce tierce. Grieve. Priest. Thieve.

(ui) Suit bruit fruit Build guilt. Juice sluice. Cruise bruise.

(aw) Aw daw haw jaw law maw paw raw saw taw chaw claw craw draw flaw gnaw shaw spaw thaw straw Bawd Sawce. Awf Awl bawl cawl mawl brawl crawl drawl spawl sprawl squawl. Hawm shawm. Dawn fawn lawn pawn sawn brawn drawn prawn thawn.

(ew) Dew few hew Jew mew new pew sew yew blew brew chew clew crew drew flew grew. knew shew skew slew stew screw shrew threw. Hew'd lewd mew'd shew'd. Hewn shewn. Bews news. Newt.

(ow) Bow low mow row sow tow blow crow flow frow glow grow know prow show slow snow stow trow scrow shrow thow. Bôw côw hôw môw nôw vôw brôw plôw Owl bowl cowl fowl howl. Own mown sown blown flown grown known shown thrown. Down gown town brown clown drown frown. Lowr, towr. Bows rows blows. Growth.

(ay) Ay bay day gay hay jay kay lay may nay pay ray say way blay bray clay dray fray gray play slay spay stay sway tray spray stray.

(ey) Hey key bey Dey grey they trey whey.

(oy) Boy coy foy joy moy noy toy. Loyd cloyd.

(uy) Buy Guy.

(eau) Beau. Beaux.

(ieu) Dieu lieu.

(iew) View.

A PRAXIS *on the* MONOSYLLABLES.

ALL Things are known to God, and tho' his Throne of State be far on high, yet doth his Eye look down to us in this low World, and see all the Ways of the Sons of Men.

If we go out, he marks our Steps. And when we go in, no Door can shut him from us. While we are by our-selves, he knows all our vain Thoughts, and the Ends we aim at: And when we talk to Friend or Foe, he hears our Words, and views the Good or Harm we do to them, or to our-selves.

When we pray, he notes our Zeal All the Day long he minds how we spend our Time, and no dark Night can hide our Works from him. If we play the Cheat, he marks the Fraud, and hears the least Word of a false Tongue.

He sees, if our Hearts are hard to the Poor, or if by Alms we help their Wants. If in our Breasts we pine at the Rich, or if we are well pleas'd with our own State. He knows all that we do, and be we where we will, he is sure to be with us.

Let us then set our-selves as in God's Sight, and look what there is in us, that he hates, and when Sin tempts us, let us stay from the Act, till we can find a Place, where his Eyes will not see us.

Bless'd are they, O Lord, who live on Earth, as in thy Sight, and have Thee in all their Thoughts: For with Thee is the Well of Life, and in thy Light fhall we fee Light.

The Lord, who made the Ear of Man,
   Muft needs hear all of right;
He made the Eye, all Things muft then
   Be plain in his clear Sight.
The Lord doth know the Thoughts of Man,
   His Heart he fees moft plain:
The Lord on high Man's Thoughts doth fcan,
   And fees they are but vain.
But, Oh! that Man is fafe and fure,
   Whom thou doft keep in Awe;
And that his Life may be moft pure,
   Doft guide him in thy Law:
For he fhall live in Peace and Reft,
   He fears not at his Death,
Love fills his Heart, and Hope his Breaft;
   With Joy he yields his Breath.

CHAP. III.

Diffyllables, or Words confifting of Two
SYLLABLES.

TABLE I.

Diffyllables accented upon the firft Syllable.

A			
AB-bot	af-ter	al-fo	ambufh
ab-ject	a-ged	al-ters	an-chor
ab-fent	a-gue	al-ways	an-gel
ac-cent	al-ley	am-ber	an-ger
ad-der	al-mond	am-ble	an-gle

an-gry	ban-ner	bi"ſket	bri-dle
an-guiſh	ban-quet	bit-ten	brief-ly
a"niſe	ban-ter	bit-ter	bri-er
an-nals	bap-tiſm	bit-tern	bright-neſs
an-ſwer	bar-bel	black-neſs	brim-ſtone
an-them	bar-ber	blank-et	bro"thel
an-tic	bar-gain	bla-zon	bro"ther
an-vil	bar-ley	ble"miſh	bru-tiſh
a-ny	bar-rel	bli"ſter	bub-ble
a-pron	bar-ren	bloo"dy	buck-et
ar-cher	bar-row	bloſ-ſoms	buck-ler
ar-den	bar-ter	blub-ber	bud-get
ar-gue	baſh-ful	blun-der	buf-fet
ar-mour	ba"ſket	blu"ſter	bul-lock
ar-my	ba-ſon	bod-kin	bul-ruſh
ar-row	ba"ſtard	bo"dy	bul-wark
a'ſpect	bat-ter	bol-ſter	bum-kin
aſſ-es	bat-tle	bond-age	bun-dle
au-dit	bai-liff	bon-grace	bur-den
au-thor	bea-con	bon-nets	bur-geſs
ax-es	bea-ver	boo-by	bur-niſh
Bab-bler	beau-ty	boo-ty	bu"ry
ba-con	beck-on	bor-der	bu"ſhel
bad-ger	bed-ſtead	bo"rough	bu"ſy
bad-neſs	beg-gar	bar-row	but-cher
baf-fle	bel-dam	bo-ſom	but-ler
bag-gage	bel-lows	bot-tle	but-ter
ba"lance	bel-ly	bot-tom	but-tock
bal-lad	ber-ry	boun-ty	but-ton
bal-laſt	be-ſom	bow-els	bux-om
bal-lot	bet-ter	brace-let	buz-zard
bal-ſam	bib-ber	bram-ble	Cab-bage
ban-dy	bi-ble	bran-diſh	cab-bin
ba"niſh	bil-lows	bra-zen	cal-dron
bank-rupt	bi"ſhop	bre-thren	cam-bric

B

ca″mel	chan-nel	cler-gy	con-teſt
cam-phire	chap-man	cli-ent	con-trite
can-cel	cha″pel	cli-mate	con-voy
can-dle	chap-lain	clo″ſet	co″ney
can-ker	chap-ter	clou-dy	coo-per
can-non	char-ger	clo-ven	cop-per
can-ton	char-ter	clo-ver	co″py
can-vas	cha ſten	clu″ſter	co″ral
ca-pon	chat-tel	clut-ter	cor-ner
cap-tain	chat-ter	cock-ney	cor-net
cap-tive	cheer-ful	cof-fee	cot-tage
car-caſs	che″riſh	cof-fin	co″ver
car-go	cher-ry	col-lar	co″vet
car-nal	cheſ-nut	col-lege	coul-ter
ca″rol	chick-en	col-lop	coun-ſel
car-pet	child-leſs	co″lours	coun-try
car-rot	child-iſh	co″lumn	cou″ple
car-ry	chil-dren	come-ly	cou″rage
caſe-ment	chim-ney	co″met	cou″ſin
caſ-tle	chi″ſel	com-fort	cow-ard
caſ-ſock	cho-ſen	com-frey	cow-ſlip
cat-tle	chur-liſh	com-mon	cox-comb
cau-dle,	ciel-ing	com-mune	crack-nels
cau-ſey	ci-pher	com-pact	craf-ty
ca″vil	cir-cle	com-paſs	creatue
ce-dar	cir-cuit	com-pound	cre″dit
cel-lar	ci″ſtern	con-cord	cri-er
cen-ſer	ci″tron	con-courſe	crim-ſon
cen-ſure	ci″ty	con-duct	cri″tic
cen-ter	ci″vet	con-duit	crook-ed
certain	ci″vil	con-flict	crot-chet
chal-lenge	cla″mour	con-quer	cru-el
cham-ber	clap-per	con-ſort	cry″ſtal
chan-cel	cha″ret	con-ſtant	cu-bit
chand-ler	cla-ry	con-ſtrue	cuck-old

cuc-kow	dea-con	dwin-dle	ex-ile
cud-gel	deb-tor	Ea-ger	Fa-ble
cul-ly	de-cent	ear-ly	fa-bric
cum-brance	de″luge	ea-gle	fac-tor
cum-min	de-fert	ear-neft	fag-got
cun-ning	dew-lap	earth-quake	fai-ry
cu-rate	di-al	eaft-ward	faith-ful
cur-dle	dif-cord	ea-fy	faith-lefs
cur-rent	dif-mal	ed-dy	fal-low
cur-ry	di″ftaff	e-dict	falf-hood
cur-tail	di″ftant	ef-fect	falf-ly
cur-tain	di″ftich	ef-fort	fal-ter
cu″ftard	di-vers	eign-ty	fa″mine
cu″ftom	diz-zy	ei-ther	fa-mous
cyg-net	doc-tor	el-bow	far-ther
cym-bal	doc-trine	el-der	far-thing
cy-prefs	dole-ful	em-ber	fa″ften
Dag-ger	dol-phin	em-pire	fa-ther
dag-gle	do-tard	em-pty	fa″thom
dain-ty	doubt-ful	end-lefs	fat-ling
dai-ry	down-ward	en-gine	fat-nefs
dal-ly	dow-ry	en-fign	faul-ty
da″mage	do″zen	en-ter	fa-vour
da″mafk	di a″gon	en-trance	fear-ful
dam-fel	di a-per	en-ti y	fea″thers
dam-fon	draw-er	en-voy	fee-ble
dan-ger	dread-ful	en-vy	field-fare
dan-driff	dri-ven	e-qual	fel-low
dark-ly	drop-fy	er-min	fc″lon
dark-nefs	drou-fy	er-rant	fe-male
dar-ling	drunk-ard	er″ror	fen-nel
dar-nel	drunk-en	e-ven	fer-ret
da″itard	dry-fhod	e″ver	fer-ry
daugh-ter	du″chefs	e-vil	fer-vent
da″zle	du-ty	eu-nuch	fet-ters

fe-ver	for-mer	gal-lant	god-defs
few-el	for-tune	gal-lon	god-head
fic-kle	for-ty	gal-lows	god-ward
fif-ty	for-ward	gal-ly	gold-en
fi"gure	foul-nefs	gam-bol	gold-fmith
fil-berd	foun-tain	gam-mon	good-ly
fil-let	four-fold	gan-der	good-nefs
fil-thy	fow-ler	gan-grene	go"fling
fin-gers	frag-ment	gar-den	go"fpel
fi"nifh	fra-grant	gar-land	got-ten
fi-nite	frank-ly	gar-lick	go"vern
fir-kin	freck-led	gar-ment	grap-ple
flab-by	free-dom	gar-ner	gran-deur
fla"gon	fren-zy	gar-nifh	gra"vel
flat-ter	fre-quent	gar-ret	gra-ver
flet-cher	friend-ly	ga"ther	grey-hound
flo-rid	friend-fhip	gen-der	great-nefs
floun-der	front-let	gen-tile	gree-dy
flou"rifh	fro-ward	gen"tle	grie"vance
flow-ers	fro-zen	ge"fture	grie"vous
flu-ent	fru-gal	gi-ant	grind-ers
flut-ter	fruit-ful	gid-dy	gri"ftle
fod-der	fru"ftrate	gil-der	griz-led
fol-low	ful-nefs	gin-ger	gro-cer
fol-ly	ful-fome	giz-zard	guilt-lefs
fool-ifh	fum-ble	glad-nefs	guil-ty
foot-man	fur-bifh	glafs-es	gun-ner
for-ces	fur-long	glean-ings	gut-ter
fore-caft	fur-nace	gli"fter	Ha"bit
fore-head	fur-nifh	glit-ter	hack-ney
fore-moft	fur-row	glo-ry	hail-ftone
fore-fhip	fur-ther	glut-ton	hai-nous
fore-fkin	fu-ry	goat-ifh	hai-ry
fo"reft	fu-ture	gob-bet	hal-bard
for-feit	Gain-ful	gob-let	hal-low

hal-ter	hem-lock	huſ-band	junc-ture
ham-mer	he″rald	hyſ-ſop	ju″ſtice
ham-per	her-ring	I-dle	Keep-er
han-dle	hew-er	i-dol	ken-nel
hand-maid	hick-up	i″mage	ker-chief
hand-ſome	hid-den	im-pulſe	ker-nel
hap-ly	high-neſs	in-cenſe	ker-ſey
hap-pen	hin-der	in-ceſt	ket-tle
hap-py	hin-ges	in-fant	kid-ney
har-bour	hire-ling	in-queſt	kin-dle
har-den	hi″ther	in-ſide	kind-neſs
har-dy	hoa-ry	in-ſtant	kin-dred
har-lot	hol-den	in-ſtinct	king-dom
harm-leſs	hol-low	in-ward	kinſ-folk
har-neſs	holp-en	irk-ſome	kinſ-man
har-per	ho-ly	i-ron	kit-chen
har-row	ho″mage	i-ſland	know-ledge
har-veſt	ho″neſt	iſ-ſue	knuc-kle
ha-ſten	ho″nour	Ja-cinth	La-bour
ha-ſty	ho″ney	jac-ket	lac-ky
hate-ful	hor-net	ja″ſper	lad der
ha-tred	hor-rour	jave-lin	la-den
ha-ven	horſe-leech	jay-lor	la-dle
haugh-ty	hoſt-age	jea″lous	la-dy
ha″vock	hot-ly	jer-kin	lam-prey
ha″zard	hou-ſes	jew-el	land-lord
ha-zle	houſ-hold	jo-cund	lan-dreſs
hea″dy	how-let	join-ture	lan-guage
heark-en	hu-man	jol-ly	lan-guiſh
hear-ty	hum-ble	jour-ney	lan-tern
hea-then	hu-mour	joy-ful	lap-wing
hea″ven	hun-dred	judg-es	large-neſs
hea″vy	hun-gry	judg-ment	laſt-ly
hei-fer	hur-ry	jug-gle	latch-et
hel-met	hurt-ful	ju-lep	late-ly

lat-ten	li″nage	mal-lows	mer-cy
lat-ter	lin-guiſt	malt-ſter	mer-maid
lat-tice	li″nen	ma″nage	mer-ry
la-ver	lin-net	man-date	meſ-ſage
lav″iſh	lin-tel	man-drake	me-tal
laugh-ter	li-on	man-ger	mid-night
law-ful	li″quor	man-gle	migh-ty
law-yer	li″ſten	man-ner	mid-wife
la-zy	lit-ter	man-tle	mil-dew
lean-neſs	li″zard	ma-ny	mil-ler
lea″ther	load-en	mar-ble	mi″mick
lea″ven	loath-ſome	mar-gin	mind-ful
le″gate	lob-ſter	mar-ket	mi″nim
lei-ſure	lo-cuſt	mar-queſs	min-ſtrel
leng″then	lof-ty	mar-row	mi″nute
len-tils	loi-ter	mar-ry	mi-ry
leo″pard	loo-ſen	mar-ſhal	miſ-chief
le″per	lo″vage	mar-tyr	mi″ſtreſs
le″prous	love-ly	mar-vel	mi-tre
leſſ-er	low-ly	ma-ſon	mix-ture
let-ters	low″ring	ma″ſter	mo″del
let-tuce	loy-al	ma-trix	mo″dern
le″vel	lo″zenge	ma-tron	mo″deſt
le-ver	lu-cre	mat-ter	moi″ſten
le-vy	luke-warm	mea″dow	moi″ſture
li-cence	lum-ber	mea-ſure	mol-ten
li-ar	lu″ſtre	med-dle	mo-ment
li-er	lu″ſty	meek-neſs	mo-ney
light-ning	luſt-ful	me″lon	mon-grel
like-neſs	lu″ſtring	mel-low	mon-key
li″ly	Mag-got	mem-ber	month-ly
lim-beck	mai-den	mem-brane	mon-ſter
lim-ber	ma″lice	men-tal	mo″ral
li″mit	mal-lard	mer-cer	mort-gage
li″mon	mal-let	mer-chant	morn-ing

mor-row	nee-dy	of-ten	pa-per
mor-fel	need-ful	oint-ment	par-boil
mor-tal	neigh-bour	oi-ſter	par-cel
mor-tar	neither	o″lives	parch-ment
mo″ther	ne″phew	o-men	par-don
mo-tive	ne″ther	on-ly	pa-rents
mot-to	net-tle	on-ward	pa″riſh
moul-dy	ne″ver	o-pen	par-lour
moun-tain	neu-ter	o″range	par-rot
mour-ner	new-ly	or-chard	par-ſly
mow-er	new-neſs	or-der	par-ſon
mud-dy	nib-ble	or-gan	par-ty
muf-fle	nig-gard	or-phan	part-ner
mul-let	nim-ble	o″ſpray	par-tridge
mum-ble	nip-ple	o″ſtrich	paſ-ſage
mur-der	no-ble	o″ther	pa″ſtor
mur-mur	noi-ſome	ot-ter	pa″ſture
mur-rain	non-ſenſe	o-ven	pa″tent
mu-ſic	non-ſuit	o-ver	pat-tern
mu″ſtard	north-ern	out-caſt	pa-tron
mu″ſter	no″ſtril	out-moſt	pave-ment
mut-ter	no-thing	out-ſide	pay-ment
mut-ton	no-tice	out-ward	pea-cock
muz-zle	nou-riſh	ox-en	pea″ſant
myr-tle	no″vice	Pad-dock	peb-ble
Na-ked	nu-ſance	pain-ful	pee-viſh
name-ly	num-ber	pa″lace	pen-ny
nap-kin	nur-ture	pa″late	pen-ſive
nar-row	nut-meg	pale-neſs	pe″nance
na-tive	Ob-ject	pal-frey	peo-ple
na-ture	o-dour	pal-let	pep-per
na-vel	of-fal	palm-tree	per-fect
naugh-ty	of-fer	pal-ſy	pe″rils
na-vy	of-fice	pam-per	pe″riſh
nee-dle	off-ſpring	pan-ther	per-ſon

pew-ter	po"plar	proud-ly	ran-cor
phan-fy	por-ter	pro-verb	ran-fom
phea"fant	po-fey	pro"vince	ra"pid
phy"fic	pof-fet	pru-dent	rafh ly
pic-ture	pot-fherd	pu"blic	ra-for
pil-grim	pot-tage	pu"blifh	ra-ther
pil-lage	pot-ter	pud-ding	rat-ling
pil-lar	poul-try	pul-pit	ra-ven
pil-low	pow-der	pu"mice	ra"vifh
pi-lot	pow-er	pu"nifh	rea"dy
pim-ple	prac-tice	pur-chafe	re-al
pin-nace	pray-er	pur-ple	rea-per
pi-per	pre-cept	pur-pofe	rea-fon
pip-kin	pre"face	Qua-drant	re"bel
pip-pen	preg-nant	quag-mire	reck-on
pi-rate	pre"late	qua-ker	re"cord
pi-ftol	pre"fence	quar-rel	red-difh
pitch-er	pre"fent	quar-ry	re"fuge
pi"ty	pret-ty	quar-ter	re"fufe
plain-nefs	prieft-hood	qua-ver	re"lic
pla"fter	prim-rofe	que-re	re"lifh
plat-ter	pri"fon	quib-ble	rem-nant
plea"fant	pri-vate	quick-ly	ren-der
plea"fure	pro-bate	quick-fand	rere-ward
plen-ty	pro"blem	qui-et	re"fcue
plow-fhare	pro"cefs	qui"ver	re"fpite
plumb-line	pro"duct	Rab-ble	re-tail
plum-met	pro"fit	rack-et	rib-band
plu-ral	pro"ject	raf-ter	rich-es
pock-et	pro"mife	rai ler	rid-dance
po-et	pro"per	rai-ment	rid-den
poi-fon	pro"phet	rain-bow	rid-dle
pol-lard	pro"fpect	rai-fins	right-ly
pom-mel	pro"fper	ral-ly	ri"gour
pon-der	pro-ftrate	ram-part	ri ot

ri″fen	fcaf-fold	fex-ton	fkir-mifh
ri″ver	fcan-dal	fhab-by	flack-nefs
rob-ber	fcarce-ly	fha″dow	flan-der
rot-ten	fcar-let	fham-bles	flaugh-ter
rough-ly	fcat-ter	fhame-ful	flen-der
roy-al	fcep-ter	fhar-pen	floth-ful
rub-bifh	fcep-tic	fhe″kel	flo″ven
ru-by	fche″dule	fhel-ter	flug-gard
rud-dy	fcho″lar	fhep-herd	flum-ber
ru-in	fci-ence	fhe″riff	fmat-ter
ru-led	fcof-fer	fhew-bread	fmit-ten
rum-mer	fcram-ble	fhip-board	fmo″ther
ru-mour	fcra-per	fhip-wreck	fno″wy
rup-ture	fcrip-ture	fhil-ling	fnuf-fers
ru-ral	fcrib-ble	fhi″ver	fo-ber
Sab-bath	fcru-ple	fhort-ly	foc-ket
fa-ble	feam-fter	fho″vel	fod-den
fack-but	fea-fon	fhoul-der	foft-ly
fack-cloth	fe″cond	fhut-tle	fo-journ
fa-crift	fe-cret	fic-kle	fo-lace
fad-dle	feem-ly	fick-nefs	fo″lemn
fad-ly	fel-dom	fig-net	fo″lid
fafe-guard	fel-ler	fi-lence	fon-net
faf-fron	fel-vedge	fil-ly	for-did
fail-or	fe″nate	fil-ver	fore-ly
fal-ly	fen-tence	fim-nel	for-rel
fam-phire	fer-jeant	fim-ple	for-row
fan-dals	fer-mon	fi″new	for-ry
fan-guine	fer-pent	fin-ful	fouth-ward
fat-chel	fer-vant	fin-gle	fpan-gle
fa-tyr	fer-vice	fir-rah	fpar-kle
fa″vage	fer-vile	fi″fter	fpar-row
fa″vour	fet-tle	fix-ty	fpeck-led
fcab-bard	fe″ven	fkil-ful	fpeech-lefs
fcab-by	fe″ver	fkil-let	fpee-dy

ſpi-der	ſtub-ble	Ta-ble	thiſtle
ſpike-nard	ſtub-born	ta-bret	thiſther
ſpin-dle	ſtuſdy	tack-ling	thought-ful
ſpiſrit	ſtum-ble	ta-ken	thou-ſand
ſpo-ken	ſtur-dy	taſlent	thral-dom
ſprin-kle	ſtur-geon	tal-low	three-fold
ſqua-dron	ſub-ject	tam-my	thrif-ty
ſquan-der	ſub-ſtance	tan-kard	thun-der
ſquir-rel	ſub-til	tan-ner	ti-dings
ſta-ble	ſub-urbs	tan-ſy	til-lage
ſtaſbliſh	ſuc-cour	ta-per	tim-ber
ſtag-ger	ſuck-ling	tap-ſter	tim-brel
ſtam-mer	ſud-den	tir-get	tinc-ture
ſtan-dard	ſu-et	tar-ry	tin-der
ſtan-za	ſuf-fer	tat-ler	tin-gle
ſta-ple	ſuf-frage	taſvern	tink-ling
ſtate-ly	ſuſgar	taw-ny	tiſ-ſue
ſtaſtue	ſul-phur	tay-lor	ti-tle
ſtaſture	ſum-mer	tem-per	tit-tle
ſtaſtute	ſun-dry	tem-peſt	to-ken
ſteaſdy	ſup-per	tem-ple	toſpic
ſted-faſt	ſure-ty	teſnant	tor-ment
ſtee-ple	ſu r-face	ten-der	tor-toiſe
ſter-ling	ſur-feit	te-net	tor-ture
ſtew-ard	ſur-name	teſnor	tor-rent
ſti-pend	ſur-plice	teſnure	to-tal
ſtir-rup	ſwag-ger	ter-ror	to-wards
ſtoſmach	ſwal-low	te-ſter	tow-el
ſto-ry	ſweet-neſs	thank-ful	tow-er
ſtor-my	ſwift-ly	there-fore	trac-tate
ſtran-ger	ſwol-len	thick-et	traf-fick
ſtran-gle	ſymp-tom	thick-neſs	tray-tor
ſtrip-ling	ſyſnod	thim-ble	tram-mel
ſtrug-gle	ſyſrup	third-ly	tram-ple
ſtrum-pet	ſyſſtem	thir-ſty	traſvel

tra″verſe	Va-cant	vo-cal	wea″pon
trea-cle	val-ley	vol-ley	wea-ry
trea-ſon	va″lour	vo″lume	wea″ther
trea″ſure	va″lue	vo″mit	wea-ſel
trea-tiſe	va″niſh	vow-el	wel-come
tre″ble	va-pour	voy-age	wel-fare
trem-ble	van-quiſh	vul-gar	whe-ther
tren-cher	var-niſh	vul-ture	whi″ſper
treſ-paſs	vaſ-ſal	Um-brag	whiſ-tle
tri-al	vel-lum	um-pire	whi″ther
tri″bute	vel-vet	un-cle	whol-ly
tric-kle	ve″nom	un-der	whol-ſome
tri-dent	ven-ture	up-per	whore-dom
tri-fle	ver-dict	up-right	wick-ed
tri″vet	ver-ger	up-roar	wi″dow
tri-umph	ve″ry	up-ward	wil-low
trod-den	veſ-ſel	ur-chin	win-dow
tro-phy	veſt-ment	ur-gent	win-now
trou″ble	ve″ſtry	u-rine	win-ter
tru-ant	ve″ſture	ut-moſt	wiſ-dom
trum-pet	vi-al	ut-ter	witch-craft
trun-dle	vi″car	Wa-fer	wi″ther
tu-lip	vic-tor	wag-gon	wit-neſs
tum-ble	vi″gil	wain-ſcot	wit-ty
tu-mour	vil-lage	wa-ken	wi″zard
tu-mult	vil-lain	wal-low	wo-ful
tur-bant	vine-yard	wan-der	wo″man
tur-nep	vint-ner	wan-ton	wo″men
tur-ret	vin-tage	war-fare	won-der
tur-tle	vi-ol	war-rant	world-ly
tu-tor	vi-per	war-ren	wor-ſhip
twen-ty	vir-gin	waſ-ſail	wor-thy
twi-light	vir-tue	watch-ful	wo-ven
twin-kle	vi″ſage	wa-ter	wrath-ful
ty-rant	vi″ſit	weak-en	wreſt-ling

wrin-kle	Yar-row	yeo"man	youth-ful
writ-ten	year-ly	yon"der	Zea-lot
wrong-ful	yel-low	young-ish	zea-lous

TABLE II.

Diffyllables accented on the latter Syllable.

A-bafe	ad-jure	a-ground	a-part
a-bate	ad-juft	a-ha	a-piece
ab-hor	ad-mire	a-larm	ap-peal
a-bide	ad-mit	a-las	ap-pear
ab-jure	a-do	a-like	ap-peafe
a-board	a-dopt	a-live	ap-plaud
a-bode	ad-vance	al-lay	ap-plaufe
a-bove	ad-verfe	al-ledge	ap-ply
a-bound	ad-vice	al-low	ap-point
a-bout	ad-vile	al-lude	ap-proach
a-broad	a-far	al-lure	ap-prove
ab-fcond	af-fair	al-moft	a-right
ab-folve	af-fect	a-loft	a-rife
ab-ftain	af-firm	a-lone	ar-raign
ab-furd	af-fix	a-long	ar-ray
ab-ufe	af-flict	a-loof	ar-rears
ac-cept	af-ford	a-loud	ar-reft
ac-cefs	af-fright	al-though	ar-rive
ac-cord	af-front	a-mend	af-cend
ac-count	a-foot	a-merce	a-fcribe
ac-crue	a-fore	a-mifs	a"fide
ac-cufe	a-fraid	a-mong	a-fleep
ac-quaint	a-frefh	a-mongft	af-fault
ac-quit	a-gain	a-mufe	af-fay
ad-here	a-gainft	a-noint	af-fent
a-dieu	a-go	a-non	af-fert
ad-journ	a-gree	a-pace	af-fefs

aſ-ſign	be-fore	be-wray	con-coct
aſ-ſiſt	be-gan	be-yond	con-cur
aſ-ſize	be-gat	blaſ-pheme	con-demn
aſ-ſume	be-get	bom-baſt	con-dole
aſ-ſure	be-gin	bri-gade	con-duce
aſ-ſwage	be-guile	buf-foon	con-fer
a-ſtray	be-half	Ca-bal	con-feſs
a-thirſt	be-held	car-bine	con-fide
at-tack	be-hind	ca-reſs	con-fine
at-tain	be-lieve	ca-reer	con-firm
at-taint	be-long	ca-ſhire	con-form
at-tempt	be-moan	ce-ment	con-found
at-tend	be-neath	cha"ſtiſe	con-front
at-teſt	be-queath	co-heir	con-fute
at-tire	be-reave	col-logue	con-geal
at-tract	be-reft	com-bine	con-join
a-vaſt	be-ſeech	com-mand	con-nive
a-venge	be-ſeem	com-mend	con-ſent
a-verſe	be-ſet	com-mit	con-ſign
a-vert	be-ſides	com-mode	con-ſiſt
aug-ment	be-ſiege	com-pare	con-ſpire
a-vail	be-ſmear	com-pel	con-ſult
a-void	be-ſought	com-pile	con-ſtrain
a-vouch	be-ſtead	com-plain	con-ſume
au-ſtere	be-ſtir	com-plete	con-tain
a-wake	be-ſtow	com-port	con-temn
a-ward	be-take	com-poſe	con-tend
a-ware	be-think	com-priſe	con-tract
a-way	be-times	com-pute	con-trive
Ba-boon	be-tray	con-ceal	con-verſe
bap-tize	be-troth	con-ceit	con-vert
be-came	be-tween	con-ceive	con-vey
be-cauſe	be-wail	con-cern	con-vict
be-come	be-ware	con-ciſe	con-vince
be-fal	be-witch	con-clude	cor-rect

I

cor-rode	de-prave	dif-patch	ex-alt
cor-rupt	de-prive	dif-penfe	ex-ceed
cou-rant	de-ride	dif-perfe	ex-cel
De-bafe	de-fcant	dif-pleafe	ex-cept
de-bate	de-fcend	dif-pute	ex-cefs
de-bauch	de-fert	dif-folve	ex-change
de-camp	de ferve	di"ftil	ex-clude
de-cay	de-fign	di"ftrefs	ex-cufe
de-ceafe	de-fire	di-veft	ex-hale
de-ceit	de- ft	di-vide	ex-hauft
de-ceive	de-fpair	di-vine	ex-hort
de-clare	de-fpife	di-vorce	ex-pect
de-cline	de-ftroy	di-vulge	ex-pel
de-cree	de-tain	E-clipfe	ex-pence
de-face	de-ter	eigh-teen	ex-pert
de-fame	de-tract	e-lect	ex-pire
de-fault	de-throne	em-balm	ex-plain
de-feat	de-vife	em-brace	ex-ploit
de-fence	de-voir	em-bofs	ex-port
de-flour	de-vote	em-ploy	ex-pofe
de-fraud	de-vour	en-camp	ex-pound
de-fray	de-vout	en-dow	ex-prefs
de-gree	dif-fufe	en-grave	ex-tend
de-ject	di-geft	en-joy	ex-tinct
de-lay	di-grefs	e-nough	ex-tol
de-light	di-rect	e-rect	ex-tract
de-lude	dif-cern	e-fcape	ex-treme
de-mand	dif-clofe	ef-chew	Fa-tigue
de-mean	dif-creet	e-fpy	fer-ment
de-mife	dif-dain	ef-fay	fo-ment
de-mur	dif-eafe	e-ftate	for-bear
de-nounce	dif-grace	wi"zard	for-bid
de-ny	dif-guife	e-vent	for-born
de-part	dif-guft	e-vert	fore-know
de-pend	dif-join	ex-act	fore-feen

fore-tel	in-flict	ob-scure	pre-sume
fore-warn	in-form	ob-serve	pre-tence
for-get	in-fringe	ob-struct	pre-vail
for-give	in-fuse	ob-tain	pre-vent
for-lorn	in-graft	oc-cur	pro-ceed
for-sake	in-join	of-fence	pro-claim
for-swear	in-nate	of-fend	pro-cure
forth-with	in-quire	op-pose	pro-duce
Gen-teel	in-rol	op-press	pro-fane
Ha"rangue	in-sert	or-dain	pro-fess
him-self	in-sist	out-run	pro-found
huz-za	in-spect	Pa-role	pro-fuse
Im-bark	in-spire	per-ceive	pro-long
im-bibe	in-stal	per-due	pro-mote
im-mense	in-struct	per-form	pro-pose
im-part	in-sult	per-fume	pro-rogue
im-peach	in-tend	per-haps	pro-tect
im-pede	in-thral	per-mit	pro-test
im-plead	in-tire	per-plex	pro-tract
im-plore	in-treat	per-sist	pro-vide
im-port	in-trench	per-suade	pro-voke
im-pose	in-vade	per-tain	pur-sue
im-pure	in-veigh	per-vert	Re-bel
im-pute	in-vent	pol-lute	re-bound
in-cline	in-volve	por-tend	re-build
in-close	La-ment	pos-sess	re-buke
in-clude	Ma-chine	pour-tray	re-cal
in-crease	main-tain	pre-cise	re-cant
in-croach	man-kind	pre-dict	re-ceipt
in-deed	ma-nure	pre-fer	re-ceive
in-dorse	ma-ture	pre-fix	re-cess
in-duce	Neg-lect	pre-mise	re-claim
in-dulge	O-bey	pre-pare	re-cord
in-fer	ob-lige	pre-sage	re-count
in-flame	ob-scene	pre-serve	re-cruit

re-deem	re-peat	re-venge	fur-prize
re-dound	re-peal	re-verfe	fur-round
re-drefs	re-pel	re-view	fuf-pect
re-fer	re-pent	re-vile	fuf-penfe
re-fine	re-pine	re-vife	fuf-tain
re-flect	re-ply	re-vive	Them-felves
re-form	re-port	re-voke	thence-forth
re-frain	re-pofe	re-volt	there-in
re-frefh	re-proach	re-ward	thir-teen
re-fund	re-proof	Sa-lute	through-out
re-fufe	re-prove	fe-cure	tor-ment
re-fute	re-pute	fe-date	tra-duce
re-gain	re-queft	fe-duce	tran"fcend
re-gard	re-quire	fin-cere	tranf-fer
re-hearfe	re-quite	fix-teen	tranf-form
re-ject	re-fent	fub-due	tranf-grefs
re-joice	re-ferve	fub-mit	tranf-late
re-lapfe	re-fide	fub-fcribe	tre-pan
re-late	re-fign	fub-fift	Vouch-fafe
re-leafe	re-fift	fub-tract	Un-clean
re-lent	re-folve	fub-vert	un-done
re-lief	re-fort	fuc-ceed	u-nite
re-ly	re-fpect	fuc-cefs	un-juft
re-main	re-fponfe	fuc-cinct	un-known
re-mifs	re-ftore	fuf-fice	un-lade
re-mit	re-ftrain	fug-geft	un-lefs
re-morfe	re-fult	fup-plant	un-loofe
re-mote	re-tain	fup-ply	un-ripe
re-move	re-tard	fup-port	un-taught
re-new	re-tire	fup-pofe	un-til
re-nounce	re-treat	fup-prefs	un-wife
re-nown	re-trieve	fur-ceafe	up-braid
re-pair	re-turn	fu-preme	up-hold
re-pay	re-veal	fur-mount	u-furp

A Praxis on the foregoing Chapter, confifting of Words not exceeding Two Syllables.

Of HEAVEN.

HEAVEN is the lofty Throne of God; but to defcribe the Glory of it is more than human Tongue can do All the Grandeur and State we behold on Earth, is not in the leaft worthy to be compar'd with it. It tranfcends all, that we are able to think. The Beauty of its Structure, the Vaftnefs of its Extent, and the Order of its Frame, are more than even our Conceits can fathom.

The Form of it is not fo much worthy our Efteem, as what it contains. There is the Prefence of God the Father, God the Son, and God the Holy Ghoft; befide great Numbers of Saints and Angels, and of Holy Men and Women, who are gone thither before us; there are Rivers of Pleafure, and Crowns of Glory.

Tho' we cannot relate the Joys of the bleffed Spirits above, yet to partake of them, and to be happy in Heaven, is the Reward of all that ive upright upon Earth. All that we can conceive, and much more, will they poffefs, who love and ferve the Lord.

That which doth further augment and enhance the Value of it, and may juftly heighten our Defires to obtain it, is, that it will laft for ever. No Time can finifh our Joys, or confume our Delights: Nothing can ever be too much to endure for thofe Pleafures that endure for ever.

Heaven is the Dwelling-Place of the Elect, the Throne of the Judge, the Seat of the Lamb, the Fulnefs of Delight, the Abode of the Juft, the Retreat of the Weary, and the Reward of the Faithful.

CHAP. IV.

Words of Three Syllables.

TABLE I.

Words accented on the First Syllable.

AB-di-cate
ab-ro-gate
ab-fo-lute
abf-ti-nence
ac-ci-dence
ac-ci-dent
ac-cu-rate
ac-ti-on
ac-tu-ate
ad-ja-cent
ad-ju-tant
ad-vo-cate
af-fa-ble
a″go-ny
al-der-man
a-li-en
a″li-ment
am-bufh-ment
a″mi-ty
am-ne-fty
a″mo-rous
an-ce″ftors
an-ci-ent
a″ni-mate
ap-pe-tite
a-pri cock

a-que-duct
a″ra-ble
ar-chi-tect
ar-gu-ment
ar-mo-ry
ar-ro-gant
ar-te-ry
ar-ti-choke
ar-ti-cle
at-tri-bute
a″va-rice
au-di-ble
au-di-ence
au-di-tor
a″ve-nue
au-gu-ry
au-tho-rize
Ba″nifh-ment
bar-ba-rifm
bar-ba-rous
bar-ri-er
bar-ri″fter
ba″fti-on
bat-te-ry
bat-tle-ment
ba″che-lor

beau-ti-fy
be″ne-fice
be″ne-fit
bi-got-ry
blun-der-bufs
bo″di-ly
boi-fte-rous
bot-tom-lefs
boun-ti-ful
bra-ve-ry
bre-vi-ty
bri-be-ry
bri″gan-tine
bro″ther-ly
bul-li-on
bur-den-fome
bur-gla-ry
bu″ri-al
bu″fi-nefs
Ca″bi-net
cal-cu-late
ca″pi-tal
cap-ti-ous
cap-ti-vate
car-di-nal
care-ful-ly

car-nal-ly	col-lo-quy	coun-te-nance
car-pen-ter	co"me-dy	coun-ter-feit
ca"ſu-al	co"mi-cal	coun-ter-pain
ca"ſu-iſt	com-fort-leſs	cour-te-ous
ca"ta-logue	com-pa-ny	cour-te-ſy
ca"te-chize	com-pe-tent	court-li-neſs
ca"val-ry	com-pli-ment	craf-ti-neſs
ca-ve-at	con-cu-bine	cre"di-ble
cau-te-rize	con-fe-rence	cre"di-tor
cau-ti-on	con-fi-dence	cri"mi-nal
ce"le-brate	con-gru-ous	cri"ti-cal
cen-tu-ry	con-ju-gal	cro"co-dile
cer-ti-fy	con-que-ror	cru-ci-fy
cham-ber-lain	con-ſci-ence	cru-di-ty
cham-pi-on	con-ſci-ous	cru-el-ty
cha-rac-ter	con-ſe-crate	cu-bi-cal
cha"pi-ter	con-ſe-quence	cu-cum-ber
cha"ri-ot	con-ſo-nant	cul-pa-ble
cha"ri-ty	con-ſta-ble	cul-ti-vate
chi"val-ry	con-ſtan-cy	cu-ri-ous
chy"mi-cal	con-ſti-tute	cu"ſhi-on
chy"mi-ſtry	con-ti-nence	cu"ſto-dy
cin-na-mon	con-tra-ry	Dam-ni-fy
cir-cu-late	con-ver-ſant	de-cen-cy
cir-cum-flex	co-pi-ous	de"di-cate
cir-cum-ſpect	co"pu-late	de-i-fy
cir-cum-ſtance	cor-di-al	de-i-ty
ci"ti-zen	cor-mo-rant	de"li-cate
cla"mo-rous	co"ro-ner	de"ni-zen
cla"ri-fy	cor-po-ral	de"pu-ty
claſ-ſi-cal	cor-pu-lent	de"pre-cate
cle"men-cy	coſt-li-neſs	de"ro-gate
co"di-cil	cot-ta-ges	de"ſo-late
cog-ni-zance	co"ve-nant	de"ſpe-rate
co"lo-ny	coun-ſel-lor	de"ſti-ny

de″sti-tute	e″le-vate	fe″ru-la
de″tri-ment	e″lo-quence	fe″sti-val
de-vi-ate	em-bas-sy	fic-ti-òn
di-a-dem	em-bry-o	fi″li-al
di-a-lect	e″me-rald	fil-thi-nefs
di-a-logue	e″mi-nent	fir-ma-ment
di-a-mond	em-pe-ror	fift″u la
di-a-per	em-pha-sis	fool-ish-nefs
di-a-ry	e″mu-late	fop-pe-ry
dif-fi-cult	e″ne-my	for-ge-ry
dif-fi-dent	e″ner-gy	for-ti-fy
dig-ni-ty	en-ter-prize	for-ward-nefs
di″li-gence	en-ti-ty	frank-in-cenfe
di-o-cefe	en-vi-ous	frau-du-lent
dif-ci-pline	e″qui-page	fruc-ti-fy
dif-fi-pate	e″qui-ty	fu-gi-tive
dif-fo-lute	e″fti-mate	func-ti-on
dif-fo-nant	e″vi-dence	fun-da-ment
do″cu-ment	ex-cel-lent	fu-ne-ral
do-na-tive	ex-cre-ment	fu-ri-ous
dow-a-ger	ex-e-cute	fur-ni-ture
dra-pe-ry	ex-er-cife	fur-ri-er
drow-fi-nefs	ex-pi-ate	fur-the″rance
du-bi-ous	ex-pli-cate	Gal-le-ry
dul-ci-mer	ex-qui-fite	gar-de″ner
dun-ge-on	ex-ta-fy	ga″ri-fon
du-pli-cate	Fa″bu-lous	ge″ne-ral
du-ra-ble	fac-ti-on	ge″ne-rate
E″bo-ny	fa″cul-ty	ge″ne-rous
e″di-fice	fal-la-cy	gen-tle-man
e″di-fy	fal-fi-ty	ge″nu-ine
e″du-cate	fa″mi-ly	gloo-mi-nefs
e″le-gant	fa″fhi-on	glu-ti-nous
e″le-ment	fe-al-ty	glut-ton-ous
e″le-phant	fer-ven-cy	gor-ge-ous

go"vern-ment
gra-ci-ous
gra"du-ate
gra"ti-tude
graf-hop-per
gun-pow-der
Hand-ker-chief
har-bin-ger
har-mo-ny
head-bo-rough
he"re"fy
he"re-tic
he"ri-tage
hi"de-ous
hin-der-moft
hi"fto-ry
ho-li-nefs
ho"mi-cide
ho"mi-ly
hor-ri-ble
huf-ban-dry
hy"po-crite
I"di-om
i"di-ot
i-dle-nefs
ig-no-ble
ig-no-rant
i"mi-tate
im-mi-nent
im-ple-ment
im-po-tent
im-pre-cate
im-pu-dent
in-ci-dent
in-di-gent

in-fa-my
in-fan-cy
in-fi-nite
in-flu-ence
in-ner-moft
in-no-cent
in-fo-lent
in-ftant-ly
in-fti-gate
in-fti-tute
in-ftru-ment
in-tel-lect
in-ter-courfe
in-te-reft
in-ter-val
in-ter-view
in-ti-mate
in-tri-cate
in-vo-cate
i"vo-ry
Jeo"par-dy
jo"cu-lar
jo-vi-al
ju"fti-fy
Ka"len-dar
kil-der-kin
kinf-wo-man
La"by-rinth
la-i-ty
lar-ce-ny
la"ti-tude
le"che-ry
le"ga-cy
le"gi-ble
le-gi-on

le"ni-ty
le"pro-fy
le"ve-ret
le"vi-ty
li"be-ral
li"ber-tine
li-o-nefs
lo"ga-rithm
lon-gi-tude
lu-na-tic
lu"fci-ous
Ma"ce-rate
ma"gi-ftrate
mag-ni-fy
ma"je-fty
main-te-nance
ma"nage-ment
ma"ni-feft
ma"ni-fold
man-fi-on
ma"nu-al
ma"nu-fcript
ma"ri-ner
mar-ma-let
mar-ti-al
mar-ve-lous
maf-cu-line
maf-fa-cre
ma"fte-ry
ma-tri-cide
me-di-ate
me"di-cine
me"di-tate
me"lo-dy
me"mo-ry

men-di-cant	night-in-gale	Pa″ci-fy
men-ftru-ous	no″mi-nate	pal-li-ate
men-ti-on	no″ta-ble	pa-pa-cy
mer-chan-dize	no″ta-ry	pa″ra-dife
mer-ci-ful	no″ti-fy	pa″ra-dox
mef-fen-ger	no″vel-ty	pa″ra-graph
mi″li-tant	nou″rifh-ment	pa″ral-lel
mil-li-on	nu-me-rous	pa″ra-phiafe
mi″ne-ral	nun-ne-ry	pa-ra-fite
mi″ni-fter	nup-ti-al	par-ri-cide
mi″ra-cle	nu-tri-ment	pa″ri-ty
mi″fe-ry	Ob-du-rate	par-ti-al
mi″ti-gate	ob-fe-quy	par-ti-cle
mo″de-rate	ob-fo-lete	paf-fi-on
mol-li-fy	ob-fta-cle	pa-ti-ence
mo″nu-ment	ob-fti-nate	pau-ci-ty
mor-ti-fy	ob-vi-ous	pe″da-gogue
mo-ti-on	o″cu-lift	pe″di-gree
moun-te-bank	o-ce-an	pe″li-can
mourn-ful-ly	o-di-ous	pe″nal-ty
mul-ti-ply	of-fi-cer	pe″ne-trate
mul-ti-tude	o″mi-nous	pe″nu-ry
mu-fi-cal	o″ni-ons	per-ju-ry
mu-ta-ble	o″pe-rate	per-pe-trate
mu-ti-ny	op-po-fite	per-qui-fite
mu-tu-al	o″pu-lent	per-fe-cute
my″ri-ad	o″ra-cle	per-ti-nent
my″fte-ry	o″ra-tor	pe″fti-lence
Nar-ra-tive	or-na-ment	pe″tu-lant
na-ti-on	or-tho-dox	pi″ge-on
na″tu-ral	of-fi-frage	pi-e-ty
na″vi-gate	o″ther-wife	pin-na-cle
naugh-ti-nefs	o-ver-fight	plen-ti-ful
neg-li-gent	out-law-ry	po-e-try
ne″ther-moft	out-ward-ly	po″li-cy

A

po"li-tic
pon-de-rous
po-pe-ry
po"pu-lar
po"pu-lous
por-ti-on
pof-fi-ble
po"fi-tive
po-ten-tate
po"ver-ty
prac-ti-cal
pre-am-ble
pre"ci-ous
pre"ci-pice
pre"ju-dice
pre"la-cy
pre"fi-dent
pre"va-lent
pre-vi-ous
pri"mi-tive
prin-ci-pal
prin-ci-ple
pri"fo-ner
pri"vi-lege
pri"vi-ly
pro-ba-ble
pro"bi-ty
pro"di-gy
pro"fli-gate
pro"ge-ny
pro"pa-gate
pro"per-ty
pro"phe-cy
pro"fe-cute
pro"fe-lyte

pro"fpe-rous
pro"fti-tute
pro"te-ftant
pro"ven-der
pfal-te-ry
punc-tu-al
pu"nifh-ment
pu-ri-fy
pu-ri-ty
pu-tri-fy
py"ra-mid
Qua-dran-gle
qua"li-fy
qua"li-ty
quan-ti-ty
que"ru-lous
que"fti-on
quint-ef-fence
quo-ti-ent
Ra-di-ant
ra"di-cal
ra-di-us
ra-pi-er
ra-ri-ty
ra"ve-nous
re"com-pence
rec-ti-fy
re"gi-cide
re"gi-ment
re-gi-on
re"gi-fter
re"gu-lar
re"me-dy
re"pro-bate
re-qui-em

re"qui-fite
re"fi-due
re"tro-grade
re"ve-rend
ri"bal-dry
righ-te-ous
ri"vu-let
roy-al-ty
ru-di-ments
ru-mi-nate
Sa"cra-ment
fa"cri-fice
fa"cri-lege
fa"la-ry
fa"li-vate
fanc-ti-fy
fa"ra-band
fa-ti-ate
fa"tif-fy
fa-vi-our
fa-vo-ry
fcor-pi-on
fcrip-tu-ral
fcru-pu-lous
fcru-ti-ny
fcul-li-on
fe-cre-cy
fec-ti-on
fe"cu-lar
fe-ni-or
fen-fu-al
fen-fi-ble
fen-fi-tive
fe"pa-rate
fe-pul-chre

se-ri-ous	suf-fra-gan	tym-pa-ny
ser-je-ant	sum-ma-ry	ty"pi-cal
ser-vi-tor	sup-ple-ment	ty-ran-nize
ser-vi-tude	sup-pli-ant	Va-can-cy
se"ve-ral	sup-pli-cant	va"cu-um
sig-ni-fy	sur-cin-gle	va"ga-bond
si'mi-le	sure-ti-ship	va"li-ant
sin-gu-lar	sur-ro-gate	va"ni-ty
si"ni-ster	su"ste-nance	va-ri-ance
si"tu-ate	sy"ca-more	va-ri-ous
slip-pe-ry	sy"co-phant	ve-he-ment
so"phi-ster	syl-lo-gism	ven-di-ble
sor-ce-ry	sym-pa-thize	ve"ne-ry
sol-di-er	sym-pa-thy	ven-ge-ance
sooth-say-er	sy"na-gogue	ve-ni-al
spa"ni-el	Te-di-ous	ve"no-mous
spe"ci-al	tem-pe-rance	ver-de-grease
spe"ci-fy	tem-po-rize	ve"ri-ly
spe"ci-men	ten-den-cy	ve"ri-ty
spec-ta-cle	ten-der-ness	ve"te-ran
spu-ri-ous	ter-ri-ble	vic-to-ry
squi-nan-cy	ter-ti-an	vic-tu-als
sta-ti-on	te"sta-ment	vi"gi-lant
stig-ma-tize	te"sti-fy	vil-lai-ny
sto"ma-cher	the-o-ry	vi"li-fy
stra"ta-gem	ti"tu-lar	vin-di-cate
straw-ber-ry	to"le-rate	vi"ne-gar
stre"nu-ous	trac-ta-ble	vi-o-late
stu-di-ous	tra"gi-cal	vi-o-lence
stu-pi-fy	trea"che-rous	vi-o-lent
sub-se-quent	tri"ni-ty	vir-gi-nals
sub-si-dy	tri"vi-al	vir-tu-ous
sub-til-ty	tur-bu-lent	vi"si-ble
suc-ces-sor	tur-pen-tine	vi"si-on
suf-fo-cate	tur-pi-tude	vi"ti-ous

vi″tri-ol	u-ni-verſe	wick-ed-neſs
Ul-ti-mate	u-ſu-al	wi″dow-er
un-der-ling	u-ſu-rer	wi″dow-hood
unc-ti-on	u-ſu-ry	wil-der-neſs
u-ni-corn	ut-te-rance	won-der-ful
u-ni-on	Way-fa-ring	work-man-ſhip
u-ni-ty	wea-ri-neſs	wretch-ed-neſs

TABLE II.

Words accented on the middle Syllable.

A-ban-don	an cho-vy	co-he-rent
a-bo″liſh	an-noy-ance	com-port-ment
a-bor-tive	a-part-ment	con-fi″ſcate
a-bun-dance	a-po″ſtate	con-jec-ture
a-bu-ſive	ap-pa″rel	con-junc-ture
ac-cep-tance	ap-point-ment	con-fi″der
ac-com-plice	ap-pren-tice	con-ſump-tive
ac-com-pliſh	aſ-ſaſ-ſin	con-tem-plate
ac-know-ledge	aſ-ſem-ble	con-tent-ment
ac-quain-tance	aſ-ſu-rance	con-ti″nue
ad-mo″niſh	a-ſto″niſh	con-tri″bute
ad-van-tage	a-ſun-der	con-tri-vance
ad-ven-ture	a-tone-ment	cor-rec-tor
ad-vi″ſing	at-ten-tive	cor-ro-ſive
ad-vow-ſon	at-tor-ney	cor-rupt-neſs
a-gree-ment	au-then-tic	De-can-ter
al-be-it	Bal-co-ny	de-cre″pit
al-low-ance	bra-va-do	de-co-rum
al-migh-ty	Ca-the-dral	de-fen-ſive
al-rea″dy	clan-de″ſtine	de-fi-ance
a-maze-ment	co-e-qual	de-lin-quent

C

de-li"ver	en-fran-chife	in-cum-bent
de-mo"lifh	en-large-ment	in-dict-ment
de-mon-ftrate	e-nor-mous	in-dul-gent
de-par-ture	en-fam-ple	in-ter-nal
de-ftruc-tive	en-vi-ron	in-for-mer
de-ter-mine	e-pif-tle	in-ha"bit
dic-ta-tor	e-fpou-fals	in-he-rent
di-mi"nifh	e-fta-blifh	in-he"rit
dif-a"fter	e-ter-nal	in-hi"bit
dif-ci-ple	ex-ac-tor	in-fi"pid
dif-co-ver	ex-a"mine	in-tan-gle
dif-junc-tive	ex-hi"bit	in-ter-nal
dif-fi"gure	ex-ph"cit	in-ter-pret
dif-ho"neft	ex-ter-nal	in-te"ftate
di-ho"nour	ex-tin-guifh	in-te"ftine
dif-plea"fure	ex-tir-pate	in-trin-fic
dif-qui-et	ex-trin-fic	in-va"lid
dif-fem-ble	Fan-ta"ftic	in-vei-gle
dif-tinct-ly	for-bear-ance	Lieu-té-nant
dif tri"bute	for-bid-den	Ma-lig-nant
di-vi-ner	Gra-na-do	ma"ri-time
di-vorce-ment	Hence-for-ward	ma-ter-nal
di-ur-nal	I-de-a	me-cha"nic
do-me"ftic	il-lu"ftrate	mif-chie-vous
E-le"ven	im-bel-lifh	Noc-tur-nal
em-bar-go	im-mor-tal	O-bei-fance
em-bez-zle	im-par-lance	ob-fer-vance
em-broi-der	im-ph"cit	oc-cur-rence
e-mer-gent	im-poft-hume	of-fen-five
em-ploy-ment	in-car-nate	out-lan-difh
en-a"mel	in-cen-tive	Pome-gra"nate
en-coun-ter	in-chant-ment	port-man-teau
en-cou"rage	in-clo-fure	por-trai-ture
en-dea-vour	in-clu-five	pre-ce-dent
e-ner-vate	in-cul-cate	pre-fump-tive

pro-hi"bit
pu-if-fant
Re-lin-quifh
re-main-der
re-mem-ber
re-mon-ftrance
re-ple"nifh
re-ple"vm
re-fem-ble
re-ti"nue
re-ve"nue
Se-du-cers
fe-que"fter
fpec-ta-tor

fub-mif-five
Tar-pau-lin
te"fta-tor
to-bac-co
to-ge"ther
tranf-pa-rent
tri-bu-nal
Vice-ge-rent
vin-dic-tive
Un-der-tain
un-co"ver
un-e-qual
un-feign-ed
un-faith-ful

un-fru-gal
un-fruit-ful
un-god-ly
un-ho-ly
un-juft-ly
un-learn-ed
un-mind-ful
un-ru-ly
un-fkil-ful
un-fta-ble
un-thank-ful
un-time-ly
un-wor-thy
u-ten-fil

TABLE III.

Words accented on the laft Syllable.

AC-qui-efce
af-ter-wards
a-la-mode
am-bu"fcade
ap-per-tain
ap-pre-hend
Cap-a-pee
ca-val-cade
cir-cum-cife
cir-cum-fcribe
cir-cum-vent
com-pre-hend
con-de-fcend

cor-re"fpond
coun-ter-mand
coun-ter-mine
coun-ter-vail
De-o-dand
dif-al-low
dif-an-nul
dif-ap-point
do"mi-neer
En-ter-tain
ex-pe-dite
Im-ma-ture
im-por-tune

in-ter-cede
in-ter-cept
in-ter-pofe
in-ter-vene
in-tro-duce
Ma-ca-roone
ma-ga-zine
maf-que-rade
O-ver-charge
o-ver-drive
o-ver-flow
o-ver-laid
o-ver-paft

o-ver-ſeer	re-in-force	there-up-on
o-ver-ſpread	ren-dez-vous	Vi-o-lin
o-ver-thrown	re″par-tee	vo″lun-teer
o-ver-whelm	re″pre-hend	Un-der-mine
Pa″ra-mount	re″pre-ſent	Where-un-to
per-ſe-vere	Se″re-nade	where-with-al
Re″col-lect	ſe″ven-teen	Ye″ſter-day
re″con-cile	There-un-to	ye″ſter-night

A PRAXIS

On the foregoing Chapter, conſiſting of Words not exceeding Three Syllables.

Of CONTENTMENT.

THink no Man happy, becauſe he outwardly appears ſo. What though Providence has largely endowed him, and Fortune ſeems fawningly to court him ; ſuppoſe him bleſt with plentiful Stores, his Subſtance daily increaſing, and every Enterprize ſucceſsful, the World affords no Joy, that he poſſeſſes not, and his Days ſeem one continued Scene of Happineſs ; yet ſtill his Bliſs may not be *Sterling*, and there may be ſome *Allay*, that may give an Abridgment to his Happineſs. His Mind may be unquiet ; many anxious Thoughts may privately gnaw upon his Vitals, and utterly overthrow the conceited Idea of Joy.

No Station in this World can afford us unmixed Pleaſures, I will therefore neither envy, nor wiſh for the Happineſs I ſee, leſt, with it, I meet thoſe Miſeries, that lie obſcure, and may bring me to Repentance for my unbounded and wanton Deſires.

All earthly Enjoyments are attended with something that mightily lessens our Joys; the Head that wears a Crown is filled with more Disquiet, than the Breast of a Commoner, and a mean Shepherd may enjoy a greater Portion of Contentment, than the wealthiest and most powerful Monarch.

If Men could plainly distinguish, and perceive the secret Misfortunes of their Neighbours, few would be desirous to change Stations with them.

O merciful God! give us the Blessing of Sedateness of Mind, then shall we be happy in every Circumstance of Life.

CHAP. V.
Words of Four Syllables.
TABLE I.
Words accented on the First Syllable.

Abro-ga-ting	com-mis-sa-ry	di"li-gent-ly
ac-cel-sa-ry	com-pe-ten-cy	Ef-fi-ca-cy
a"gri-mo-ny	com-pa-ra-ble	e"le-gan-cy
a"la-ba"fter	com-pli-ca-ted	e"li-gi"ble
a-li-e-nate	con-fi"fto-ry	e"vi-dent-ly
al-le-go-ry	con-ti-nen-cy	ex-cel-len-cy
a-mi-a-ble	con-tro-ver-fy	ex-em-pla-ry
a"mi-ca-ble	con-tu-ma-cy	ex-o-ra-ble
an-ti-qua-ry	cor-ri-gi-ble	Fi"gu-ra-tive
ar-bi-tra-ry	cor-pu-len-cy	for-mi-da-ble
Be"ne-fit-ing	cor-rup-ti-ble	Ge"ne-ral-ly
Ca"ter-pil-lar	co"vet-ouf-nefs	glo-ri-ouf-ly
ce"re-mo-ny	cu-ri-ouf-ly	Ha"ber-dafh-er
cha"ri-ta-ble	De"li-ca-cy	he"te-ro-dox
com-for-ta-ble	de"fpi-ca-ble	ho"nou-ra-ble

C 3

Words of Four Syllables.

ho''fpi-ta-ble	Na''tu-ral-ly	fo-ci-a-ble
Ig-no-mi-ny	na''vi-ga-ble	fo''li-ta-ry
in-no-cen-cy	ne''cef-fa-ry	fum-ma-ri-ly
in-ven-to-ry	ne-cro-man-cy	Ta''ber-na-cle
ju-di-ca-ture	O''ra-to-ry	tem-po-ral-ly
La''pi-da-ry	Pa-tri-mo-ny	te''fti-mo-ny
le-gif-la-tive	pe-remp-to-ry	to''le-ra-ble
li''be-ral-ly	pre-mu-ni-re	tranf-i-to-ry
Ma''le-fac''tor	pur-ga-to-ry	tri''bu-ta-ry
mar-vel-louf-ly	Ra-ti-o-nal	tur-bu-len-cy
ma''tri-mo-ny	rea-fon-a-ble	Va''li-ant-ly
me''lan-cho-ly	re-frac-to-ry	va-ri-a-ble
me''mo-ra-ble	right-e-ouf-nefs	ve''ge-ta-ble
mer-ce-na-ry	Sa''la-man-der	ve-he-ment-ly
mi''li-ta-ry	fanc-tu-a-ry	ve''ne-ra-ble
mi''fe-ra-ble	fe''cre-ta-ry	vir-tu-ouf-ly
mo-de-rate-ly	fe''pa-ra-tift	vi''gi-lan-cy
mo''na-fte-ry	fe''ve-ral-ly	vo''lun-ta-ry

TABLE II.

Words accented on the Second Syllable.

AB-bre-vi-ate	ad-mi''ni-fter	al-le-gi-ance
a-bi''li-ty	ad-mif-fi-on	al-lu-fi-on
a-bo''mi-nate	ad-op-ti-on	am-baf-fa-dor
a-bun-dant-ly	ad-ver-ten-cy	am-bi''gu-ous
ac-ce''le-rate	ad-ver-tife-ment	am-bi-ti-on
ac-cef-fi-ble	a-dul-te-rate	am-phi''bi-ous
ac-com-mo-date	af-fec-ti-on	a-na''lo-gy
a-ci''di-ty	af-flic-ti-on	a-na''ly-fis
ac-ti''vi-ty	af-fi''ni-ty	a-na''to-mize
ad-di-ti-on	a-la''cri-ty	a-na''to-my

an-ge"li-cal	ca-no"ni-cal	con-ca"vi-ty
an-ni-hi"late	ca-pa"ci-ty	con-cep-ti-on
an-ti"qui-ty	ca-pi"tu-late	con-clu-ſi-on
an-ti"pa-thy	ca pri"ci-ous	con-cu-piſ-cence
a-po"ca-lypſe	cap-ti"vi-ty	con-cuſ-ſi-on
a-po"lo-gy	ce-le"ri-ty	con-di"ti-on
a-po"ſta-ſy	ce-le"ſti-al	con-fec-ti-on
a-po"ſta-tize	cen ſo-ri-ous	con fe"de-rate
a-po"ſto-lic	cen-tu-ri-on	con-feſ-ſi-on
ap-pa"ri-tor	cer ti"fi-cate	con for-mi-ty
ap-pel-la-tive	ceſ-ſa-ti-on	con-fu-ſi-on
ap-pro-pri-ate	cha me-le-on	con-gra"tu-late
ap-pur-te-nance	chi-rur-ge-on	con-gru-i-ty
ar-bi"tra-ment	cir-cum-fe-rence	con-junc-ti-on
ar-ti"cu-late	col-la"te ral	con-ſpi"cu-ous
ar-ti"fi-cer	col-la-ti-on	con-ſpi"ra-cy
ar-til-le-ry	col-lec-ti-on	con-ſpi"ra-tor
a"ſper-ſi-on	col-le-gi-ate	con-ſtruc-ti-on
aſ-ſaſ-ſi-nate	com-bu"ſti-ble	con-ſump-ti-on
aſ-ſi"du-ous	co-me-di-an	con-ta-gi-on
aſ-ſo-ci-ate	com-me"mo rate	con-ta"mi-nate
aſ-ſump-ti-on	com-miſ-ſi-on	con-ten-ti-on
at-ten-ti-on	com-mo-di-ous	con-ti"nu-ance
at-te"nu-ate	com-mo"di-ty	con-trac-ti-on
au-da-ci-ous	com-mu-ni-cate	con-tri"ti-on
au-tho"ri-ty	com-mu-ni-on	con-ve-ni-ent
Bar-ba-ri-an	com-pa"ni-on	con-ver-ſi-on
bar-ba"ri-ty	com-paſ-ſi on	con-vic-ti-on
be-a"ti-fy'd	com-pen di-ous	con-vul-ſi-on
be-a"ti-tude	com-pe"ti-tor	cor-po-re-al
be ha-vi-our	com-plex-i-on	cor-rec-ti-on
be-ne"fi-cence	com-po"ſi-tor	cor-ro"bo-rate
be-ne"vo-lence	com-preſ-ſi-on	cor-rup-ti-on
bi-tu-mi-nous	com-pul-ſi-on	cre-a-ti-on
Ca-la"mi-ty	com-punc-ti-on	cre-du-li-ty

Dam-na-ti-on	diſ-tinc-ti-on	ex-a″ſpe-rate
de-bi″li-ty	di-ver-ſi-ty	ex-clu-ſi-on
de-cen-ni-al	di-vi″ſi-on	ex-em-pli-fy
de-ci″ſi-on	Ef-fec-tu-al	ex-emp-ti-on
de-coc-ti-on	ef-fe″mi-nate	ex-hi-la-rate
de-fec-ti-on	ef-fi″ci-ent	ex-o″ne-rate
de-fi″ci-ent	ef-flu vi-um	ex or-bi-tant
de-ge″ne-rate	ef-fu-ſi-on	ex-pan-ſi-on
de-jec-ti-on	e-gre-gi-ous	ex-pe-di-ent
de-lec-ta-ble	e-jec-ti-on	ex-pe-ri-ence
de-li″be-rate	e-la″bo-rate	ex-pe″ri-ment
de-li″ci-ous	e-lec-ti-on	ex-po″ſi-tor
de-li″ne-ate	e-ma″ſcu-late	ex-preſ-ſi-on
de-li′ver-ance	em-broi-de″rer	ex-pul-ſi-on
de-lu-ſi-on	e-miſ-ſi-on	ex-te″nu-ate
de-mo-ni-ac	em-pha-ti-cal	ex-te-ri or
de-po″pu-late	en-co-mi-um	ex-tor-ti-on
de-preſ-ſi-on	en-thu-ſi-aſm	ex-trac-ti-on
de-ri″ſi-on	e-nor-mi-ty	ex-tra-va-gant
de-ſcrip-ti-on	e-pi″ſco-pal	ex-tre″mi-ty
de-ſer-ti-on	e-pi″to-mize	ex-u-be-rant
de-ſtruc-ti-on	e-qua″li-ty	Fa-ci″li-ty
de-ter-mi-nate	e-qui″va-lent	fal-la-ci-ous
de-trac-ti-on	e-qui″vo-cal	fa-mi″li-ar
de-vo-ti-on	e-qui″vo-cate	fan-ta″ſti-cal
dex-te″ri-ty	e-ra″di-cate	fe-ro″ci-ty
dif-fu-ſi-on	er-ro-ne-ous	fer ti″li-ty
di-greſ-ſi-on	e rup ti-on	fe″ſti″vi-ty
di-men-ſi-on	eſ ſen ti-al	fi-de″li-ty
di-mi″nu-tive	e-ter-ni-ty	foun-da-ti-on
di-rec-ti-on	e-the-re-al	fra-gi″li-ty
dif-cre″ti-on	e-va″cu-ate	fru-i″ti-on
dif-cuſ-ſi-on	e-va″po rate	Gar-ru-li-ty
diſ-ho″ne-ſty	e-va-ſi on	gram-ma″ti-cal
diſ ſen-ſi-on	ex-ac-ti-on	Har-mo-ni-ous

hu-ma″ni-ty	in-fec-ti-ous	Má-gi″ci-a
hu-mi″li-ty	in-fe-ri-or	mag-ni″fi-cence
hy-dro″pi-cal	in-ge-ni-ous	ma-le″vo-lent
hy-po″cri-ſy	in-he″ri-tance	ma-li″ci-ous
hy-po″the-ſis	i″ni-qui-ty	ma-te-ri-al
I-den-ti-ty	i″ni″ti-ate	ma-tri″cu-late
i-do″la-trous	in-junc-ti-on	ma-tu-ri-ty
il-li″te-rate	in-ju-ri-ous	me-lo-di-ous
il-lu-mi-nate	in-ſcrip-ti-on	me-ri″di-an
il-lu″ſtri ous	in-ſcru-ta-ble	mi-li″ti-a
im-ma″cu-late	in-ſi″nu-ate	mor-ta″li-ty
im-me-di-ate	in-ſpec-ti-on	mu-ni″fi-cent
im-mer-ſion	in-ſtruc-ti-on	mu-ſi″ci-an
im-mu-ni-ty	in-te″gri-ty	Nar-ra-ti-on
im-mu-ta-ble	in-tel-li-gence	na-ti″vi-ty
im-par-ti-al	in-ten-ti-on	no-bi″li-ty
im-pe″di-ment	in-te-ri-or	no-to-ri-ous
im-pe-ri-ous	in-va-ſi-on	O-be-di-ence
im per-ti-nent	in-ven-ti-on	ob-jec-ti-on
im-pe″tu-ous	in-ve″te-rate	ob-la-ti-on
im-pla-ca-ble	in-vi-o-late	ob-li″te-rate
im-por-tu-nate	in-vi″ſi-ble	ob-li″vi-on
im-po″ve-riſh	i-ro″ni-cal	ob-nox-i-ous
im-preſ-ſion	ir-re″gu-lar	ob-ſcu-ri-ty
im-pu-ni-ty	ir-re″ve-rent	ob-ſtruc-ti-on
in-ceſ-ſant-ly	ir-rup-ti-on	oc-ca-ſi-on
in-ci″ſi-on	Ju-di″ci-al	œ-co″no-my
in-con-gru-ous	ju-di″ci-ous	of-fi″ci-ous
in-cor-po-rate	La-bo-ri-ous	om-ni″po-tent
in-de″fi-nite	laſ-ci″vi-ous	om-ni″ſci-ent
in-de″li-ble	le-gi″ti-mate	o-pi″ni-on
in-dem-ni-fy	li-cen-ti-ate	op-preſ-ſi-on
in-dem-ni-ty	li-cen-ti-ous	op-pro-bri-ous
in-du″ſtri-o u	lieu-te″nan-cy	o-ra-ti-on
in-ef-fa-ble	li-ti″gi-ous	o-ri″gi-nal

out-ra-ge-ous	pro-di"gi-ous	ſa-ti-e-ty
Par-ti"cu-lar	pro-feſ-ſi-on	ſe-cu-ri-ty
par-ti"ti-on	pro-ge"ni-tor	ſe-di"ti-on
pa-the"ti-cal	pro-por-ti-on	ſe-ve"ri-ty
pa-vi"li-on	pro-pri-e-ty	ſi-mi"li-tude
pe-cu-li-ar	pro"ſpe"ri-ty	ſim-pli"ci-ty
pe-nu-ri-ous	pro-vin-ci-al	ſin-ce"ri-ty
per-di"ti-on	pro-vi"ſi-on	ſo-bri-e-ty
per-fec-ti-on	punc-ti"li-o	ſo-ci-e-ty
per-fi"di-ous	pur-ga-ti-on	ſo-lem-ni-ty
per-ni"ci-ous	Qua-ter-ni-on	ſub-jec-ti-on
per-pe"tu-al	quo-ti"di-an	ſub-miſ-ſi-on
per-plex-i-ty	Re-bel-li-on	ſub-ſcrip-ti-on
per-ſpi"cu-ous	re-cep-ta-cle	ſub-ſer-vi-ent
per-ſua-ſi-on	re-cep-ti-on	ſub-ſtan-ti-al
pe-ti"ti-on	re-ci"pro-cal	ſub-trac-ti-on
phi-lo"ſo-pher	re-demp-ti-on	ſub-ver-ſi-on
phy-ſi"ci-an	re-din-te-grate	ſuc-ceſ-ſi-on
pol-lu-ti-on	re-flex-i-on	ſuf-fi"ci-ent
poſ-ſeſ-ſi-on	re-ge"ne-rate	ſta-bi"li-ty
po-ſi"ti-on	re-jec-ti-on	ſu-pre"ma-cy
po"ſte"ri-ty	re-i"te-rate	Tau-to"lo-gy
po"ſti"li-on	re-la-ti-on	tem-pe"ſtu-ous
po-ten-ti-al	re-li"gi-on	ter-re"ſtri-al
pre-ci"pi-tate	re-luc-tan-cy	tra-di"ti-on
pre-de"ſti-nate	re-miſ-ſi-on	tran-quil-li-ty
pre-dic-ti-on	re-ſpon-ſi-ble	tranſ-greſ-ſi-on
pre-do"mi-nate	re-ſto"ra-tive	tranſ-la-ti-on
pre-e"mi-nence	re-ſtric-ti-on	tri-en-ni-al
pre-pa"ra-tive	re-ten-ti-on	tu-i"ti-on
pre-po"ſte-rous	re-ta"li-ate	tu-mul-tu-ous
pre-ro"ga-tive	rhe-to"ri-cal	ty-ran-ni-cal
preſ-by"te-ry	ri-di"cu-lous	Va-ca-ti-on
pre-ſcrip-ti-on	Sa-ga"ci-ty	va-cu-i-ty
pre-ſump-tu ous	ſal-va-ti-on	ve-ne-re-al

1

ve-ra″ci-ty	vic-to-ri-ous	U-bi″qui-ty
ver-mi″li-on	vir-gi″ni-ty	un-cer-tain-ty
vex-a-ti-on	vi-va″ci-ty	un-righ-te-ous
vi-cif-fi-tude	vo-lup-tu-ous	ux-o-ri-ous

TABLE III.

Words accented on the Third Syllable.

A″da-man-tine	ma-ra-ve-dis
af-fi-da-vit	me″lan-cho″lic
a-gri-cul-ture	me-mo-ran-dum
a″na-bap-tift	mif-ad-ven-ture
ap-pre-hen-five	me-ta-mor-phofe
ar-bi-tra-tor	No-men-cla-tor
Bar-ri-ca-do	Om-ni-pre-fent
Co-ad-ju-tor	or-na-men tal
com-pre-hen-five	Pa-tro-ny″mic
cor-re-fpon-dent	pe-do-bap-tifm
Dif-in-he″rit	per-ad-ven-ture
dif-con-ti″nue	per-fe-ve-rance
For-ni-ca-tor	pre-de-cef-for
How-fo-e″ver	Sa-cer-do-tal
In-ter-lo-per	fu-do-ri″fic
in-ter-mix-ture	fup-ple-men-tal
Ma-the-ma″tics	Who-fo-e″ver

On the laft Syllable.

Le″ger-de-main	Ne″ver-the-lefs

A PRAXIS

On the foregoing Chapter, consisting of Words not exceeding Four Syllables.

Of RELIGION.

A School-Boy, entering upon his Learning, imagines it a Work of great Difficulty, that it will require Abundance of Labour and Care, that the Procedure must cost him much Pains, beside the Fear of losing many and delightful Hours of Play. He is very loth to begin; all the Persuasions, Advice, or Threatenings of his Master are irksome to him, but as he proceeds further, and perceives the Advantages, which he will gain by good Tuition, it appears with a more delightful Prospect; he will relinquish all Joys and youthful Sports to arrive at some Perfection in Learning; each Author affords him new Delights, and therein he places his chiefest Contentment.

So it is with most Men. Being advised to a religious Course, they imagine it a terrible Task impossible to be undergone, and that they shall never go through with it; that it will rob them of all their darling Pleasures, and deprive them of all their beloved Enjoyments. This makes them very loth to set about it, they think it too severe, and full only of Austerity; the Way seems very rugged and troublesome, and they are unwilling to travel in that Path; but if they once conquer the Reluctancy of their sensual Appetites, and overthrow their Obstructions; if they but once begin to be sensible of the pernicious Confequences of their Miftake, thence-forward they meet the moft ravifhing Delights. Then Religion feems truly pleafant and agreeable, Practice removes the Difficulty, and makes the dreaded Labour eafy; they would not then quit their prefent State for all the tranfitory Enjoyments the World can afford. Then they acknowledge, that its Beginning only is laborious, its Continuance pleafant, and its End the trueft Felicity.

N B. See more Leffons in the Appendix.

C H A P. VI.

Words of Five Syllables.

T ABLE I.

Words accented on the Second Syllable.

A-bo"mi-na-ble
 am-bi"ti-ouf-ly
a-po"the-ca-ry
aux-i"li-a-ry
Com mu-ni-ca-ble
con-fec-ti-o-ner
con-fe'de-ra-cy
con-temp-tu ouf-ly
con-ti"nu-al-ly
con-tri"bu-ta-ry
con-ve-ni-en-cy
Dif-cre"di-ta-ble
Ef-fi"ci-en-cy
e-gre-gi-ouf-ly
e-fpe"ci-al-ly
ex-tor-ti-o-ner

ex-tra"va-gan-cy
ex-u-be-ran-cy
Har-mo-ni-ouf-ly
he-re"di-ta-ry
Im-me-di-ate-ly
in-cen-di-a-ry
in-con-ti-nen-cy
in-cor-rup-ti-ble
in-e"vi-ta-ble
in-ex-o-ra-ble
in-i"mi-ta-ble
in-nu-me-ra-ble
in-fu-pe-ra-ble
ir-re"pa-ra-ble
ir-re"vo-ca-ble

Laf-ci″vr-ouf-nefs
le-gi″ti-ma-cy
No-to-ri-ouf-ly
O-ri″gi-nal-ly
Pe-cu-ni-a-ry
per-pe″tu-al-ly
pro-tho″no-ta-ry

Re-po″fi-to-ry
Un-ne″cef-fa-ry
un-rea-fon-a-ble
un-mea-fu-ra-ble
un-pro″fi-ta-ble
un-righ-te-ouf-nefs
un-fe″pa-ra-ble

TABLE II.

Words accented on the middle Syllable.

AB-di-ca-ti-on
a″ca-de″mi-cal
ac-cep-ta-ti-on
ac-qui-fi″ti-on
ad-mi-ra-ti-on
ad-mo-ni″ti-on
a″do-ra-ti-on
a″du-la-ti-on
af-fa-bi″li-ty
af-fec-ta-ti-on
al-le-ga-ti-on
al-le-go″ri-cal
am-bi-gu-i-ty
am-mu-ni″ti-on
am-pu-ta-ti-on
a″na-the″ma-tize
a″ni-mo″fi-ty
an-ni-ver-fa-ry
an-no-ta-ti-on
ap-pa-ri″ti-on

ap-pel-la-ti-on
af-fi-du-i-ty
a″ftro-lo″gi-cal
a″ftro-no″mi-cal
a″va-ri″ci-ous
Be-a-ti″fi-cal
be″ne-dic-ti-on
be″ne-fi″ci-al
Ca″fti-ga-ti-on
ce″le-bra-ti-on
ce″re-mo-ni-al
cir-cu-la-ti-on
cir-cum-ci″fi-on
cir-cum-fpec-ti-on
co-ef-fen-ti-al
com-bi-na-ti-on
com-mi-na-ti-on
com-pe-ti″ti-on
com-pre-hen-fi-ble
com-pre-hen-fi-on

con-de-ſcen-ſi-on	dif-o-be-di-ent
con-fla-gra-ti-on	dif-pen-ſa-ti-on
con-fu-ta-ti-on	dif-po-ſi"ti-on
con-gre-ga-ti-on	dif-ſo-lu-ti-on
còn-ju-ra-ti-on	di"ſtri-bu-ti-on
con-ſe-cra-ti-on	di"vi-na-ti-on
con-ſo-la-ti-on	do"mi-na-ti-on
con-ſtel-la-ti-on	E"du-ca-ti-on
con-ſter-na-ti-on	ef-fi-ca-ci-ous
con-ſti-tu-ti-on	e"lo-cu ti-on
con-ſul-ta-ti-on	e"mu-la-ti-on
con-tem-pla-ti-on	e"pi-de"mi-cal
con-tra-dic-ti-on	e-qua-ni-mi-ty
con-tri-bu-ti-on	e"ſti-ma-ti-on
con-tu-ma-ci-ous	ex-com-mu-ni-cate
con-tu-me-li-ous	ex-e-cra-ti-on
con-ver-ſa-ti-on	ex-e-cu-ti-on
co"pu-la-ti-on	ex-ha-la-ti-on
co"ro-na-ti-on	ex-hi bi"ti on
cor-po-ra-ti-on	ex-hor-ta-ti-on
De"cla-ma-ti-on	ex-pec-ta-ti-on
de"cla-ra-ti-on	ex-pe-di"ti-on
de"di-ca-ti-on	ex-pi-ra-ti-on
de"fa-ma-ti-on	ex-pla-na-ti-on
de"fi-ni"ti-on	ex-po-ſi"ti-on
de-mo-cra"ti-cal	Fer-men-ta-ti-on
de-mon-ſtra-ti-on	for-ni-ca-ti-on
de"po-ſi"ti-on	Ge"ne-ra-ti-on
de"pri-va-ti-on	ge"ne-ro"ſi-ty
de"pu-ta-ti-on	Ha"bi-ta-ti-on
de"ri-va-ti-on	he"ſi-ta-ti-on
de"ſo-la-ti-on	ho"ſpi-ta"li-ty
de"ſpe-ra-ti-on	hy"po-cri"ti-cal
de-va"ſta-ti-on	Il-le-gi"ti-mate
di-a-bo"li-cal	im-be-ci"li-ty

i"mi-ta-ti-on   op-por-tu-ni-ty
im-po-fi"ti-on   op-po-fi"ti-on
in-cli-na-ti-on   or-di-na-ti-on
in-cor-rup-ti-on   o"ften-ta-ti-on
in-di-vi"du-al   Par-ti-a"li-ty
in-flam-ma-ti-on   per-pen-di"cu-lar
in-qui-fi"ti-on   per-pe-tu-i-ty
in-fpi-ra-ti-on   per-fe-cu-ti-on
in-fti-tu-ti-on   per-fpi-cu-i-ty
in-fur-rec-ti-on   per-tur-ba-ti-on
in-ter-cef-fi-on   pe"fti-len-ti-al
in-tro-duc-ti-on   pof-fi-bi"li-ty
in-vi-ta-ti-on   pre"pa-ra-ti-on
Ju-rif-dic-ti-on   pre"fer-va-ti-on
La-men-ta-ti-on   prin-ci-pa"li-ty
li"be-ra"li-ty   pro"cla-ma-ti-on
li"mi-ta-ti-on   pro"di-ga"li-ty
Ma-gi"fte-ri-al   pro-hi-bi"ti-on
mag-na-ni"mi-ty   pro"pa-ga-ti-on
ma"the-ma"ti-cal   pro"ro-ga-ti-on
me-di-o"cri-ty   pro"vi-den-ti-al
me-di-ta-ti-on   pro"vo-ca-ti-on
mi"ni-ftra-ti-on   pub-li-ca-ti-on
mif-con-ftruc-ti-on   pu-fil-la"ni-mous
mo"de-ra-ti-on   pu-tre-fac-ti-on
mul-ti-pli"ci-ty   Quint-ef-fen-ti-al
mu-ta-bi"li-ty   Re"col-lec-ti-on
Na"vi-ga-ti-on   re"for-ma-ti-on
non-con-for-mi-ty   re-lax-a-ti-on
nu-me-ra-ti-on   re"no-va-ti-on
Ob-li-ga-ti-on   re"pe-ti"ti-on
ob-fer-va-ti-on   re"pre-hen-fi-on
oc-cu-pa-ti-on   re"pro-ba-ti-on
o-do-ri"fe-rous   re"pu-ta-ti-on
o"pe-ra-ti-on,   re"fer-va-ti-on

re″ſo-lu-ti-on
re″ſto-ra-ti-on
re″ſur-rec-ti-on
re″tri-bu-ti-on
re″ve-la-ti-on
re″ve″ren-ti-al
re″vo-lu-ti-on
Sa″cri-le-gi-ous
ſa″lu-ta-ti-on
ſa-tiſ-fac-ti-on
ſe″pa-ra-ti-on
ſin-gu-la″ri-ty
ſi″tu-a-ti-on
ſpe″cu-la-ti-on
ſuf-fo-ca-ti-on
ſu-per-fi″ci-al
ſu-per-ſcrip-ti-on

ſu-per-ſti″ti-on
ſup-pli-ca-ti-on
ſup-po-ſi″ti-on
ſur-rep-ti″ti-ous
Te″ſti-mo-ni-al
to″le″ra-ti-on
tranſ-por-ta-ſi-or
tri″bu-la-ti-on
Va″le-dic-ti-on
va-ri-a-ti-on
ve″ge-ta-ti-on
ve″ne-ra-ti-on
vin-di-ca-ti-on
vi-o-la-ti-on
Un-ad-vi-ſed-ly
u-ni-for-mi-ty

A PRAXIS

On the foregoing Chapter, conſiſting of Words not exceeding Five Syllables.

Of MAN.

Ord, what is Man! Originally Duſt, ingen-
dred in Sin, brought forth with Sorrow,
helpleſs in his Infancy, extravagantly wild in his
Youth, mad in his Manhood, decrepit in his
Age; his firſt Voice moves Pity, his laſt com-
mands Grief.

Nature clothes the Beaſts with Hair, the Birds
with Feathers, and the Fiſhes with Scales; but
Man is born naked, his Hands cannot handle,
his Feet cannot walk, his Tongue cannot ſpeak,
nor his Eyes ſee aright; ſimple his Thoughts,

vain his Defires, Toys his Delights. He no
fooner puts on his diftinguifhing Character REA-
SON, but he burns it with wild-fire Paffions,
taints it with abominable Pride, tears it with
infatiable Revenge, dirts it with Avarice, and
ftains it with Debauchery!

His next State is full of Miferies. Fears torment, Hopes intoxicate, Cares perplex, Ene-
mies affault him, Friends betray him, Thieves
rob him, Wrongs opprefs him, and Dangers
way-lay him

His laft Scene is deplorable; his Eyes dim,
Hands feeble, Feet lame, Sinews fhrunk, Bones
dry, his Days are full of Sorrow, his Nights
of Pain, his Life miferable, his Death terrible:
his Infancy is full of Folly, Youth of Diforder
and Toil, Age of Infirmity!

Lord, what is Man! A Dunghil blanched
with Snow, a May-game of Fortune, a Mark
for Malice, a Butt for Envy! If Poor, defpi-
fed; if Rich, flattered, if Prudent, miftrufted;
if Simple derided! his Beauty is but a Flower, his Strength, Grafs; his Wit, a Flafh; his
Wifdom, Folly; his Judgment, weak; his Art,
Imperfection; his Glory, a Blaze, his Time, a
Span; himfelf, a Bubble! He is born Crying,
lives Laughing, and dies Groaning!

Who then to vain Mortality fhall truft,
But limns the Water, or but writes in Duft!

CHAP. VII.

Words of Six and Seven Syllables.

The Accent is upon the Third Syllable from the End, unless otherwise marked.

AB-bre-vi-a-ti-on
a-bo-mi-na-ti-on
ac-com-mo-da-ti-on
ad-mi-ni-ftra-ti-on
a"ni-mad-ver-fi-on
an-ni-hi-la-ti-on
an-nun-ci-a-ti-on
ar-chi-e-pi"fco-pal
a"ri-fto-cra"ti-cal
af-faf-fi-na-ti-on
af-fe-ve-ra-ti-on
af-fo-ci-a-ti-on
Ca"pi-tu-la-ti-on
ce-re-mó-ni-ouf-ly
cir-cum-lo-cu-ti-on
cir-cum-vo-lu-ti-on
co-ef-fen-ti-a"li-ty
com-me-mo-ra-ti-on
com-mu-ni-ca-ti-on
con-fi-de-ra-ti-on
con-fub-ftan-ti-a-ti-on
con-ti-nu-a-ti-on
cor-ro-bo-ra-ti-on
De-li-be-ra-ti-on
de-li-ne-a-ti-on
de-no-mi-na-ti-on

de-ter-mi-na-ti-on
di-la"pi-da-ti-on
dif-ad-van-ta-ge-ous
dif-con-ti-nu-a-ti-on
dif-fi-mu-la-ti-on
Ec-cle-fi-a"fti-cal
e"di-fi-ca-ti-on
e-ja-cu-la-ti-on
e"lee-mó"fy-na-ry
en-thu-fi-a"fti-cal
e-qui-vo-ca-ti-on
e-ra-di-ca-ti-on
é-va-cu-a-ti-on
e-va-po-ra-ti-on
ex-a-mi-na-ti-on
ex-a"fpe-ra-ti-on
ex-com-mu-ni-ca-ti-on
ex-po"ftu-la-ti-on
ex-te"nu-a-ti-on
ex-tra-or-di-na-ry
Fa-mi-li-a"ri-ty
for-ti-fi-ca-ti-on
fruc-ti-fi-ca-ti-on
Ge-o-grá"phi-cal-ly
glo-ri-fi-ca-ti-on
gra-ti-fi-ca-ti-on

He″te″ro-ge-ne-ous
hu-mɪ″lɪ-a-tɪ-on
I″ma″gɪ-na-ti-on
im-mu-ta-bɪ″lɪ-ty
ɪn-fal-li-bɪ″lɪ-ty
in-ſen-ſi-bɪ″lɪ-ty
in-ter-pre-ta-tɪ-on
in-ter-ro-ga-tɪ-on
ir-re-gu-la″rɪ-ty
Ma-the-ma-tɪ″ci-an
mo″dɪ″fi-ca-ti-on
mor-tɪ″fi-ca-ti-on
mul-tɪ″plɪ-ca-tɪ-on
Na″tu-ra″lɪ-za-tɪ-on
O-be-di-en-ti-al
Pre-de″ſtɪ-na-ti-on
pro-cra″ſti-na-tɪ-on
pro-nùn″ci-a-tɪ-on
pro-pi″ti-a-tɪ-on

pro-pór-ti-o-na-ble
pu-rɪ-fi-ca-tɪ-on
pu-ſil-la-nɪ″mɪ-ty
Qua″lɪ-fi-ca-tɪ-on
Ra″tɪ″fi-ca-tɪ-on
re-ca-pɪ″tu-la-tɪ-on
re″com-men-da-ti-on
re″con-cɪ″li-a-tɪ-on
re-ge″ne″ra-tɪ-on
re″pre-ſen-ta-tɪ-on
re-ta″lɪ-a-tɪ-on
Sanc-ti-fi-ca-tɪ-on
ſig-nɪ-fi-cā-ti-on
ſo-lem′-nɪ-za-ti-on
ſu-pe-rɪ-o″rɪ-ty
Tranſ-fi″gu-ra-ti-on
tran-ſub-ſtan-ti-a-ti-on
Un-cir-cum-cɪ″ſi-on
u-nɪ-ver-ſa″li-ty

A P R A X I S

On the foregoing Chapter, conſiſting of ſome Words
of ſix Syllables.

Early P I E T Y.

THAT Travéller is unqueſtionably more
likely to accompliſh his Journey, that ſets
out betimes in the Morning, than he that lin-
gers till the Sun's Declination   A great deal of
Pains muſt be uſed to regain the Minutes that
are fled; which, had they been well employed,
that Labour had been ſaved.   It requires more
indefatigable Labour to recover waſted Time,

than beneficially to improve it, when prefent.
The Hazards are infinite, the Difficulties extraordinary; and vaftly difproportional are the
Odds that may attend Delay. He that defers
the Works of Piety till ripe Years, or old Age,
is very uncertain of fecuring his Salvation. Evil
Habits are not foon put off; having once taken
Root they are not eafily fupplanted, or perhaps
Time may not be allowed; for the Abufe of
God's Mercy is no Warrant for the Continuation of it, and much more remains to be performed in an Inch of Time, than need to have
been done in our whole Span. Humiliation for
paft Tranfgreffions is a Work indifpenfably neceffary, but a careful Obedience lightens the
Burden, and facilitates the Tafk, to the Performance of which there is no Method fo rationally
effectual as to begin young. An early Piety is
a great Step toward walking in the Paths of
Goodnefs; and a *Child, trained up in the Way that
he fhould go, will not depart from it when he is
old.* Lord, water us in the Spring with the Dew
of Heaven, that at the univerfal Harveft of the
World, thou may gather us into thy Paradifaical Garner !

Some have died young, while others old have fell;
Yet thofe liv'd long enough, who lived well.

CHAP. VIII.

*Proper Names, and Words usually written
with a Capital Letter at the Beginning.*

TABLE I.

Words of One Syllable.

AI Aix Anne, Bath Bede Bell Blan Bench
Boyn Boys Briel Buz, Caen Cain Charles
Chrift Cis Claude Cleves Crete Cufh; Dan Dane
Delft Diep Dort Dutch; Elb Er Eve; Fez
France French Fulk; Gad Gath Gaul George
Ghent God Greece Greek Guife; Hague Hou
Hugh Hull Hur; Jah James Jane Jew Joar
Job John Jove Joice Jude June; Kent Kir Kifh
Koz, Lifle Lot Luke Luz Lyn; Maefe Mark
Mars May Mede Mentz Metz Meufe Mons;
Nants Ner Nice Nile Nob Nod Noph; Og
Owze, Pau Paul Phut Pierce Pul Pur; Ralph
Reu Rhine Rhodes Rhone Roan Rome Ruth
Rye; Saul Scot Seine Seir Seth Shaul Shem
Shur Spain Spire Swede; Thames Thebes Toul
Tours Trent Troy Turk Tweed Tyre; Ur
Uz, Wales Ware Wells Wilts Worms; York;
Zair Ziph Ziz Zouch Zug Zuph Zur Zuvd.

TABLE II.

*Proper Names of Two Syllables, having the
Accent on the First Syllable.*

A-ron	A-phek	Ba-lak	Ce-dron
Ab-ba	A-pril	Bal-tic	Ce-phas
A-bel	A-ram	Ba-rak	Ce-far
Ab-ner	Ar-kite	Ba-ruch	Chal-dees
A-chifh	Ar-nold	Ba-fhan	Chat-ham
A-chor	Ar-non	Bed-ford	Che-rub
Ach-fah	A-fa	Bed-lam	Chil-mad
A"dam	A-faph	Be-rith	Chim-ham
Ad-vent	Afh-dod	Ber-nard	Chi-na
A-gag	A-fher	Be"ryl	Chi"flu
A"gate	Afth-ma	Beth-el	Chit-tim
A-gur	A"thens	Beth-fhan	Chy"mift
A-hab	Au-guft	Bil-dad	Chrift-mas
A-haz	Au-tumn	Bil-hah	Cle"ment
Al-bert	A-ven	Bif-cay	Cli-mate
Al-fred	A"vims	Bla"ftus	Co-logn
Al-gum	A-vites	Blen-heim	Con-clave
Al-mug	A-vith	Bo-za	Co-os
A"loes	Az-buck	Bo-tolph	Cor-ban
Al-pha	A-zem	Boz-rah	Co-rinth
Al-phage	Az-mon	Bri"ftol	Coz-bi
Am-mon	A-zure	Bri"tain	Cu-fhan
Am-non	A-zez	Ca"defh	Cu-fhi
A-mos	Az-zah	Ca"lais	Cy-clops
Am-ram	Ba-al	Ca-leb	Cy-prus
A-nak	Ba-bel	Cam-bridge	Cy-rus
An-drew	Bak-buk	Car-mel	Da-gon
An-nas	Ba-laam	Ca"ftor	Da-niel

Da"nube	E-li	Go-fhen	I-faac
Da-than	El-len,	Gui"nea	In-dies
Da-vid	En-dor	Ha-dad	Ipf-wich
De-bir	En"glifh	Ha-gar	Ja-bal
De-dan	E-noch	Hag-gai	Jab-bok
Del-phos	E-nos	Ha-man	Ja-bin
De-mas	E-phod	Ha-mor	Ja-cob
Den-bigh	E-phron	Ha-ran	Ja-el
Der-be	E-fau	He-ber	Jam-bres
Der-by	Efh-col	He-brew	Jan-nes
Di-bon	Ef-rom	He-bron	Ja-phet
Di-nah	Ef-fex	Hec-tic	Ja-fon
Do-eg	Ef"ther	He-ge	Je-hu
Dor-cas	E-tham	Hen-ry	Jeph-thah
Do-than	E"thics	Her-mes	Jef-fe
Dub-lin	Eu-rope	Her-mit	Je-fus
Dun-kirk	Ez-ra	Her-mon	Je-thro
Dur-ham	Fal-mouth	He-ro	Jo-ab
Ea"fter	Fe-lix	He"rod	Jo-afh
E-bal	Feu-wick	Hert-ford	Jo-bab
E-ber	Fe"ftus	Hin-nom	Jo-el
E"cho	Fran-ces	Hoch-ftet	Jok-tan
Ec-logue	Fran-cis	Hol-land	Jo-nas
E-den	Fri-day	Ho-mer	Jop-pa
Ed-mund	Ga-al	Hoph-ni	Jo-feph
E-dom	Ga-za	Ho"race	Jo-tham
Ed-ward	Ge-ber	Ho-reb	Ju-bal
Ed-win	Ger-man	Hum-ber	Ju-dah
Eg-bert	Ger-fhom	Hum-phrey	Ju-das
Eg-lon	Ge-fhur	Hu"fhi	Ju-dith
E-gypt	Ge-zer	Hu-fhim	Ju-ly
E-hud	Gil-bert	Hu-zoth	Ju"ftus
E-kron	Gil-gal	Hy-dra	Ka-defh
E-lam	God-win	Hy-men	Ke-dar
El-dad	Go-mer	Hy-phen	Kei-lah

Ke-nite	Mar-tha	Om-ri	Rab-bi
Ki-son	Ma-ry	O-nan	Ra-ca
Kit-tim	Mat-than	O-nyx	Ra-chel
Ko-hath	Mat-thew	O-phir	Ra-hab
Ko-rah	May-or	O"phrah	Ra-mah
La-ban	Med-way	Op-tics	Reu-ben
La-chish	Me-shech	O-reb	Ri"chard
La-mech	Mi-cah	Or-nan	Rim-mon
La"tin	Mi"lan	O"vid	Riz-pah
Lau"rence	Mil-cah	Ox-ford	Ro"bert
Le-ah	Mil-dred	Oz-ni	Ro"ger
Leo"nard	Mo-ab	Pa-dan	Ro-mans
Let"tice	Mo-loch	Pam-phlet	Row-land
Le"vi	Mo"narch	Pa"nic	Ru-fus
Le-vite	Mon-day	Pa"ris	Sa-lem
Lew-is	Mon-mouth	Pa"shur	Sal-mon
Lib-nah	Mo-ses	Pe-ka	Sam-son
Lin-coln	Muf-ti	Pe-leg	Sap-phire
Lis-bon	Na-bal	Pem-broke	Sa-rah
Litch-field	Na-both	Pe-ter	Sar-dine
Lo"gic	Na-dab	Phan-tasm	Sar-dis
Lon-don	Na-dir	Pha-rez	Sa-tan
Lu-cy	Na-hor	Phe-nix	Sa-turn
Lyd-da	Na-hum	Phi"lip	Sa"voy
Ly"ric	Na-ples	Pi-late	Se-lah
Ly"stra	Na-than	Pi-rate	Se"vern
Ma-chir	Ne-bat	Pis-gah	Sha-drach
Ma"dam	Ne-cho	Pla"net	Shal-lum
Ma-dan	Nec-tar	Pri"sca	She-chem
Ma"gic	Nim-rod	Pro-logue	Shit-tim
Ma-gog	No-ah	Pro"vost	Shu-hite
Mam-mon	Nor-man	Psal-mist	Shu-shan
Mam-re	Nor-wich	Pu-dens	Si-mon
Man-na	O-bed	Quin-tus	Si-nai
Mar-quis	O-mer	Rab-bah	Si-on

D

Smyr-na	Tar-fhifh	Tuef-day	Ze-nith
So"dom	Tha-mar	Ty-rus	Ze-red
South-wark	Tho"mas	Vafh-ti	Zi-ba
Staf-ford	Thum-mim	Ve-nice	Zig-lag
Ste-phen	Thurf-day	U-rim	Zil-pah
Sto-ic	Ti-tus	Uz-zah	Zim-ri
Suc-coth	To-bit	Wal-ter	Zi-on
Sun-day	To-paz	War-wick	Zip-por
Ta-bor	To-phet	Xer"xes	Zo-phar
Ta'lent	Tri-bune	Za-dok	Zo-an
Tan-gent	Tu-bal	Zal-mon	Zo-ar

Words accented on the latter Syllable.

'A'dage	Co-lofs	Ju-ly	O-ftend
A-men	E"fquire	Ma-drid	Stock-holm
Car-lifle	Hoch-ftet	Mo-gul	Thou-lon
Ca-tarrh	Ja-pan	Na-varre	

TABLE III.

Proper Names of Three Syllables.

Accented on the Firft Syllable.

A"bi-gal	Ad-mi-ral	A"ma-lek
A'bi-fhag	A'fri-ca	A"ma-fa
A"bi-fhat	A"ga-bus	A"me-thyft
A-bi-ud	Al-chy-mift	A"na-gram
A-bra-ham	Al-ge-bra	A"nar-chy
Ab-fa-lom	Al-mo-dad	An-gle-fey

An-gli-cifm
An-ti-chrift
An-ti-och
An-ti-pas
A-ntho-ny
A"pho-rifm
A-qui-la
A-re-tas
Ar-ra-gon
Ar-te-mas
Afh-ke-lon
Au-ftri-a
Bac-cha-nals
Ba"by-lon
Bar-ba-ry
Bar-na-bas
Ba"ro-net
Bar-fa-bas
Ba"fi-lifk
Bath-fhe-ba
Bdel-li-um
Be-li-al
Ben-ja-min
Be"tha-ny
Beth-le-hem
Beth-pha-ge
Beth-fhe-mefh
Bi"ga-my
Bo-ni-face
Buck-ing-ham
Cai-a-phas
Ca-na-an
Can-da-ce
Can-ti-cle
Ca-pri-corn

Car-bun-cle
Car-me-lite
Ca"ta-ract
Ca"te-chifm
Ca-tho-lic
Chan-cel-lor
Chan-ce-ry
Che"ru-bim
Chi"che"fter
Cho"co-late
Chri"fti-an
Chro"ni-cle
Chry-fo-lite
Chry"fo"ftom
Clau-di-us
Cle-o-phas
Col-che-fter
Co"lo-nel
Con-ftan-tine
Cor-fi-ca
Cy"pri-an
Da"ma-ris
Da"ni-el
De"bo-rah
De"ca-logue
De"li-lah
De"von-fhire
Di"dy-mus
Do-na-tift
E"din-burgh
E"do-mites
E"kro-nites
E"la-mites
E-li-ab
E-li-hu

E"li-phaz
El-ka-nah
E"ly-mas
E"me-rald
E"pa-phras
E-phra-im
E"pi-cure
E"pi-logue
E"thel-bert
Eu-cha-rift
E"ve-rard
Eu-lo-gy
Ex-e-ter
Ex-o-dus
Ex-or-cifm
Fre"de-ric
Gab-ba-tha
Ga-bri-el
Ga"li-lee
Gal-lo-way
Ge"ne-fis
Ge"no-a
Ger-ma-ny
Gi"be-ah
Gi"de-on
Gi"le-ad
Glou-ce"fter
Gol-go-tha
Gre"go-ry
Ha"vi-lah
Ha"za-el
He"mi-fphere
Hep-tar-chy
He"re-ford
Ho"ro-fcope

Hu-go-not	Ly"ci-a	Pass-o-ver
Hun-ga-ry	Ly"di-a	Pa"ta-ra
Hun-ting-ton	Ly"si-as	Pa-tri-arch
I-ro-ny	Mach-pe-lah	Pa"tro-bas
Ish-bo-sheth	Mag-da-len	Pen-te-cost
Ish-ma-el	Ma-ho-met	Pe"nu-el
Is-ra-el	Ma"la-chi	Per-ga-mos
Is-sa-char	Man-tu-a	Per-si-ans
I"ta-ly	Mar-ga-ret	Pha"nu-el
Je"bu-site	Mar-ge-ry	Pha"ri-sees
Je"su-ite	Me-di-a	Phi"li"stines
Je"shu-run	Me"le-a	Phi"ne-has
Je"ze-bel	Me"li-ta	Phry"gi-a
Jez-re-el	Mer-cu-ry	Pon-ti-us
Jo-a-chim	Me"ta-phor	Por-tu-gal
Jo"na-dab	Mid-dle-sex	Po"ti-phar
Jo"na-than	Mr"ri-am	Pres-by-ter
Jo"sa-phat	Mo-a-bite	Pro"cho-rus
Jos-ce-lin	Mo"de-na	Pub-li-can
Jo"shu-a	Mor-de-cai	Pu-ri-tan
Ju-bi-lee	Mu"sco-vy	Rab-sha-keh
Ju-da-ism	Na-a-man	Ram-me-lies
Ju-li-us	Na-o-mi	Ro"che-ster
Ju-pi-ter	Naph-ta-li	Ro"ge-lim
Kad-mi-el	Na"za-reth	Ro"la-mord
Ka"len-dar	Na"za-rite	Sad-du-cees
Ka"tha-rine	Ni"co-las	Sa"la-min
Ke"mu-el	Ni"ne-veh	Sa"mu-el
Ko-ha-thit	Nor-man-dy	San-he-drim
La"za-rus	Not-ting-ham	Sa"tur-day
Le"ba-non	O"be-lisk	Sax-o-ny
Lei-ce"ster	O-pi-um	Sce"le-ton
Le-mu-el	Oth-ni-el	Se-ra-phim
Lu-ci-fer	Pa"la-tine	Shi"me-i
Lu-ci-us	Pa"le-stine	Shrews-bu-ry

Shu-na-mite	Te"ma-nite	Whit-ſun-tide
Si"ci-ly	Te"na-riff	Wil-li-am
Si"me-on	Ter-ri-er	Win-che"ſter
Si"ſe-ra	Ti"mo-thy	Wi"ni-fred
So"do-mite	The-o-dore	Woı-ce-ſter
So"lo-mon	Tu"ſca-ny	Xe"no-phon
Sof-the-nes	Tv"chi-cus	Zab-di-el
Swit-zer-land	Va"len-tine	Za"cha-ry
Syl-ve"ſter	Va"ti-can	Za"re-phath
Sy"ri-ans	U-ri-el	Ze"be-dee
Ta"bi-tha	Uz-zi-el	Ze"bu-lun
Tai-ta-ıy	Wed-neſ-day	Zip-po-rah
Te-ko-ah	Weſt-min-ſter	Zo-di-ac
Te"le-ſcope		

TABLE IV.

The Accent is upon the Second Syllable in the following Words.

A-bad-don	Au-gu"ſtus	Cho-ra-zin
A-bi-a	A-zo-tus	Co-ni-ah
A-bi-hu	Ba-rab-bas	Cy-re-ne
A-bi-ram	Bar-je-ſus	Da-ma"ſcus
A-cro"ſtic	Bar-jo-na	Da-ri-us
A-dul-lam	Bar-zil-lai	De-cem-ber
A-grip-pa	Bel-ſhaz-zar	Di-a-na
A-hi-jah	Ben-ha-dad	Di-lem-ma
A-hi-tub	Ber-ni-ce	Ec-lip-tic
A-po"ſtate	Be-theſ-da	E-li-as
A-po-ſtle	Biſ-ſex-tile	E-li-jah
Ap-pen-dix	Chal-de-a	E-li-ſha
Arch-an-gel	Chi-me-ra	E-qua-tor

D 3

E-raſ-mus	Mat-thi-as	Sa-lo-me
E-ra″ſtus	Me-ra-ri	San-bal-lat
E-ſai-as	Meſ-ſi-as	Sap-phi-ra
Eu-ni-ce	Mi-le-tum	Sa-rep-ta
Eu-phra-tes	Na-aſ-ſon	Sep-tem-ber
Ge-ha-zi	Ni-ca-nor	Su-ſan-na
Ge-ne-va	No-vem-ber	Syl-va-nus
Ge-ri-zim	Oc-to-ber	Ter-tul-lus
Go-li-ah	O-lym-pic	Teu-to″nic
Go-mor-rah	O-me-ga	Thad-de-us
Ha-bak-kuk	O-ri-on	To-bi-as
Hil-ki-ah	O-zi-as	Try-phe-na
Ho-ri-zon	Phe-ni-ce	Try-pho-ſa
Ho-ſan-na	Phi-le-mon	Vi-en-na
Ho-ſe-a	Phi-le-tus	U-phar-ſin
Je-ho-ram	Phi″lip-pi	U-ri-ah
Je-ho-vah	Priſ-cil-la	Uz-zi-ah
Jo-ſi-as	Re-be″kah	Zac-che-us
Ju-de-a	Sa-be-ans	Zal-mu-na
Ke-tu-rah	Sal-mo-ne	Ze-bo-im
Ma-naſ-ſeh		

TABLE V.

Words accented on the laſt Syllable.

A″ber-deen	Ca″mi-ſar	Ca″va-lier
Am-ſter-dam	Ca-pu-chin	Cla″ien-cieux
	Ca″ra-van	In-gol-ſtad
Buc-a-niers		

TABLE VI.

Words of Four Syllables, that have the Accent on the First Syllable.

A"lex-an-der Hi-e-rar-chy Pa"ne-gy"ric
 Can ter-bury Ja"ni-za-ry Pe-ter-bo"rough
Fe"bru-ary Kid-der-min-ster Sa"lif-bu-ry

Words accented on the Second Syllable.

A-bed-ne-go	Be-za-le-el	E-ly"fi-um
A-bi-a-thar	Ca-per-na-um	Em-ma"nu-el
A-bi"me-lech	Ca-ta"ftro-phe	En-thu-fi-afm
A-bi"na-dab	Ce-fa-re-a	E-pe"ne-tus
A-bi"no-am	Chro-no"lo-gy	E-phe-fi-ans
A-cel-da-ma	Ci-li"ci-a	E-van-ge-lift
A-cha-i-a	Co-lof-fi-ans	Eu-ro"cly-don
A-chi"to-phel	Cor-ne-li-us	E-ze-ki-el
A-mi"na-dab	Cof-mo"gra-phy	Ga-la-ti-a
A-na"the-ma	Cy-re-ni-us	Ga-ma-li-el
A-po"cry-pha	Dal-ma-ti-a	Gen-ne-fa-ret
A-pol-ly-on	De-ca"po-lis	Ge-o"gra-phy
An-ti"pa-tris	De-me-tri-us	Geth-fe"ma-ne
A-ra-bi-a	De-mo"cra-cy	Her-mo"ge-nes
A-rith-me-tic	Di-a"go-nal	He"ro-di-as
Ar-me-ni-a	Di-a"me-ter	Hy-dro"gra-phy
Ar-mo-ni-ac	Di-o"ge-nes	Hy-per-bo-le
A"ftro"no-my	Di-o"tre-phes	I-co-ni-um
A"ftro"lo-gy	E-bed-me-lech	Il-ly"ri-cum
A"fyn-cri-tus	E-gyp-ti-an	I-ta"li-an
Bar-tho"lo-mew	E-li-a-kim	Je-hoi-a-da
Ba-va-ri-a	E-li"me-lech	Je-hoi-a-kim
Be"tha"ba-ra	E-li"za-beth	Je-ho"na-dab
Be"thu-li-a		

D 4

Je-ho"sha-phat	Pa-la"ti-nate	So-si"pa-ter
Je-ru-sa-lem	Pam-phy"li-a	The-o"do-lite
Le-vi-a-than	Phi"lip-pi-ans	The-o"phi-lus
Le-vi"ti-cus	Phi"li"sti-a	Ti-be"ri-us
Ly-sa-ni-as	Phle-bo"to-my	Ti-mo-the-us
Me-he-ta-bel	Phy-lac-te-ry	Tro-gyl-li-um
Mel-chi"ze-dek	Po-ly"ga-my	Ve"spa-si-an
Me-phi"bo-sheth	Po-ti"phe-ra	Vice chan-cel-lor
Mer-cu-ri-us	Quin-ti"li-an	Vi-tel-li-us
Me-thu-se-lah	Sa-la-thi-el	U-ra-ni-a
Me-tro"po-lis	Sa-ma"ri-tans	U-to-pi-a
Mont go"me-ry	Sar-di-ni-a	West-pha-li-a
Na-tha"ni-el	Se-mi-ra-mis	Xe-no"cra-tes
Ne-a"po-lis	Sen-na"che"rib	Ze-lo"phe-had
Ni-co"po-lis	Se-ra"gli-o	Ze-no-bi-a
O-lym-pi-ad	Si"gi-o-noth	Ze-rub-ba-bel
O-ne"si-mus	Si-le-sia	Zi-do-ni-ahs

TABLE VII.

Proper Names of Four Syllables having the Accent on the Third Syllable.

A bi-e-zer	A"za-ri-ah	E"be-ne-zer
A-bi-le-ne	Ba-ra-chi-as	E-le-a-zar
A"do-ni-jah	Bar-ce-lo-na	E-li-e-zer
A"ma-de-us	Bar-ti-me-us	For-tu-na-tus
A"na-bap-tist	Be-er-she-ba	Ge"da-li-ah
A"na-ni-as	Bel-te-shaz-zar	Ha"cha-li-ah
An-dro-ni-cus	Bo-a-ner-ges	Ha"de-re-zer
A"ri"star-chus	Ca"te-chu-men	Hal-le-lu-jah
Ar-ta"xer"xes	Co-pen-ha-gen	Ha"na-ni-ah
A"tha-li-ah	Dal-ma-nu-tha	He"ze-ki-ah
At-ta-li-a	Di-a-pa-son	I-du-me-a

I-tu-re-a	Mi-ti-le-ne	Shal-ma-ne-zer
Je"co-ni-ah	Na"zi-an-zen	She"ca-ni-ah
Je"re-mi-ah	Ne-he-mi-àh	Sta"nif-la-us
Je"ro-bo-am	Ni"co-de-mus	The-o-do-rus
Ke-he-la-thah	O"ba-di-ah	Thy-a-ti-ra
La"dif-la-us	O-bed-E-dom	Tra-"cho-ni-tis
Ma-ha-na-im	Pi-ha-hi-roth	Ze"ba-di-ah
Mat-ta-thi-as	Pto"le-ma-is	Ze"chi-ri-ah
Me-ne-la-us	Re-ho-bo-am	Ze"de-ki-ah
Me-ri-o-neth	Sa"ra-gof-fa	Ze"pha-ni-ah

TABLE VIII.

Proper Names of Five and Six Syllables.

Note, *The Accent is upon the laft Syllable but two.*

A-bel-beth-ma-a-cha	E"ty-mo"lo-gy
A-dra-myt-ti-um	E-van-ge"li-cal
An-da-lu-fi-a	E-vil-me"ro-dach
A"pol-lo-ni-a	Ge-ne-a"lo-gy
A"ri-fto"cra-cy	Ge-o-gra"phi-cal
Be-ro-dach-Ba"la-dan	He-li-o"po-lis
Cap-pa-do-ci-a	Hi-e-ra"po-lis
Ca"ta-lo-ni-a	Hi"fto-ri-o"gra-phy
Che-dor-la-o-mer	Ho-mo-ge-ne-ous
Chri"fti-a"nity	Hy-per-bo"li-cal
Deo-te"ro"no-my	Li-thu-a-ni-a
Di-o-ny"fi-us	Ly-ca-o-ni-a
Ec-cle-fi-a"fti-cus	Ma"ce-do-ni-a
E-nig-ma"ti-cal	Ma-ha-la-le-el
E-qui-noc-ti-al	Me-di"ter-ra-ne an
E-thi-o-pi-a	Me-fo-po-ta-mi-a

Me-tro-po″li-tan
Na-bu-za″ra-dan
Ni-co-la-ı-tan
O-ne-ſi″pho-rus
Phi-la-del-phi-a
Phy″ſi-og-no-my
Sa-mo-thra-ci-a

Scan-di-na-vi-a
The-o-lo″gi-cal
Theſ-ſa-lo-ni-ans
Tra-gi-co″me-dy
Tran-ſyl-va-ni-a
U-ni-ver-ſi-ty

TABLE IX.

Words accented on the laſt Syllable but one.

A-bel-Miz-ra-im
A-do″ni-be-zek
A-do″ni-ze-dek
A-ha-ſu-e-rus
Al-mon-Dib-la-tha-im
A-re-o-pa-gite
A-rı″ma-the-a
A-riſ-to-bu-lus
Ba-al-pe-ra-zim
Con-ſtan-ti-no-ple
Ec-cle-ſi-a″ſtes
E-pa″phro-di-tus
E″pi-cu-re-an

Ge-de-ro-tha-im
Hy-po-chon-dri-ac
La-o-di-ce-a
Ma-gor-miſ-ſa-bib
Ma-her-ſha-lal-haſh-baz
Me-ſhe-le-mi-ah
Mı″di-a-ni-tiſh
Ne-bu-chad-nez-zar
Ne-bu-chad-rez-zar
Prog-noſ-ti-ca-tor
Theſ-ſa-lo-ni-ca
Tob-a-do-ni-jah
Zaph-nath-pa-a-ne-ah

A GUIDE

To the ENGLISH TONGUE.

PART II.

CHAP. I.

Of Letters in General.

The MASTER. The SCHOLAR.

M. HOW is the *Alphabet* divided?

S. The whole *English Alphabet*, containing twenty-six Letters, is divided into *Vowels* and *Confonants.*

M. What is a *Vowel?*

S. A *Vowel* is a Letter, that makes a full and perfect Sound of itfelf, without which there can be no *Syllable.*

M. How many *Vowels* are there?

S. There are five *Vowels*; a, e, i, o, u.

M. Is not y a *Vowel* fometimes?

S *Y* is a *Vowel*, when it follows a *Confonant*, and founds like *i*; as, *by, reply.*

M. How many *Confonants* are there?

S. The other twenty-one Letters are *Confonants*, fo called, becaufe, they make no *Sound* nor *Syllable*, without the Help of a *Vowel.*

M. What is a *Syllable?*

D 6

S. A *Syllable* is the Sound of a *Vowel* or *Diphthong,* either with, or without Confonants; as, *a, an, and, rand, ftrand.*

M. What is a *Diphthong?*

S, A *Diphthong* is the Meeting of two *Vowels* in one and the fame *Syllable*

Note, *I call it the* Meeting *only, and not the* Sound *of two* Vowels, *according to the true and proper Notion of a* Diphthong; *because in many of them, one of the* Vowels *is not at all pronounced.*

M. How many *Diphthongs* are there?

S There are twelve *Diphthongs,* ai, ei, oi, and ui; au, eu, ou, ee, oo, ea, oa, and ie.

Note, *That at the End of Words we ufe* y *and* w *to conclude the* Diphthongs, *inftead of* i *and* u, *without varying the Sound, which produces feven that are called* improper Diphthongs, *namely,* ay, ey, oy, *and* uy; aw, ew, *and* ow.

M What is a *Triphthong?*

S. A *Triphthong* is the Meeting of three *Vowels* in one *Syllable*; as, *eau* in Beau, Beauty; and *ieu* in lieu, adieu.

M What mean you by a long *Syllable?*

S. A long *Syllable* is, when a *fingle Vowel* is at the End of it; or when it is followed with *b, gh, gm, gn, ll;* or *e final*; or laftly, when there is a *Diphthong* in it.

M. Give fome *Examples.*

S. A-bâ-fed; ah, fê-lah, hîgh, high-er; phlêgm, sîgn-ing; re-câll-ed; a-rîfe, de-fpîfe; ftrai-ner, a-maîn, Sea, Gui"nea, Queen, feen, &c.

Note 1. *Sometimes* e Final *is added, and the* Sylla-ble *founded fhort, as may be feen in the Obferva-tions upon that* Letter.

2 *Sometimes also the* Diphthongs *are pronounced short; as may be seen in the Table of* Monosyllables *(where they are also marked) and in the Observations upon them, in the* Third Chapter *following*

M. What is meant by a short *Syllable?*

S. A short *Syllable* is that which ends with one or more *Consonants.*

M. Give some Examples of short *Syllables.*

S. Băd-nĕss, rŭd-der, sĭn-fŭl, fŏr-mer, slŭt-tish.

CHAP. II.

Remarks on the Sound of particular Letters, and of those which are usually left out in Pronunciation.

A.

M. HOW many *Observations* have you of the Letter *a?*

S. I have Three *Observations* of the Letter *a.*

M. Give the *First*

S. A is not sounded in these Words, *Pharaoh* (Pháro) *marriage* (márrige) *carriage* (cárrige) *chaplain* (cháplin) *Parliament* (Párliment).

M. Give the *Second.*

S. Most of the *Proper Names,* that have *aa,* drop one of them in the Pronunciation; as, *Isaac* (Izác) *Canaan* (Cánan) *Balaam* (Bálam) except *Ba-al,* and *Ga-al.*

M. Give the *Third.*

S. A is sounded broad like *aw,* in all Words before *ld* or *ll*; as, *báld, scáld; Báll, cáll,* &c. and in *Wáter.*

B.

M. Give me an Account, in what Words the Letter *b* is written, but not founded.

S. *B* is not founded in these Words following, *debt* [det] *debtor* [détter] *fubtle* [futtle] *doubt* [dout] *dumb* [dum] *thumb* [thum] *crumb* [crum] *plumb* [plum] *lamb* [lam] *limb* [lim].

M. In what Words does *b* ferve to lengthen the *Syllable?*

S. *B*, like *e* final, lengthens the *Syllable* in *climb* [clime] *comb* [come] *womb* [wome] *coxcomb* [coxcome].

C.

M. Hath *c* always one and the fame Sound?

S The ancient *Saxons* always founded it hard like *k*; but we pronounce it oftentimes foft like *s*.

M. When is *c* to be founded hard?

S. *C* is hard like *k*, before *a*, *o*, *u*, and the Confonants *l*, *r*; as, *came*, *clay*, *corn*, *crab*, *cub*.

M. When is *c* to be founded foft?

S. *C* is foft like *s*, before *e*, or *i*, and *y*; as, *cement*, *city*, *tendency*. Except *Aceldama*; and *Cis*, which is otherwife written *Kifh*.

M How is *fc* founded?

S. When *fc* comes before *e* or *i*, the *c* is quite foft; as, *fcene*, *fcience*. Except that it is founded hard in *fceptic*, *fcepticifm*, *Scæva*, *fceleton*.

M. What Words are there in which *c* is not founded?

S *C* before *k* is quite foft; as, *back*, *quick*.

It is alfo loft in thefe Words, *Schifm* [fizm] *verdict* [vérdit] *indictment* [inditement] *victuals* [víttles] *victualler* [vítler] *perfect* [pérfit] *perfected* [pérfited] *perfectnefs* [pérfitnefs] but it is founded in *Perfection*, *perfective*.

M. When is *ch* founded like *k*?

S. Ch is founded like *k* in moſt foreign Words, eſpecially in the proper Names of the *Holy Bible*; as *Chymiſt, Choler, Baruch, Archippus, Melchiſedec, Archangel.*

M. Are not ſome particular Words excepted?

S. The ancient *Engliſh* Sound of *ch* is uſually retained in theſe Words, *Arch, Archbiſhop, Archdeacon, Architect, Rachel, Cherubim, Stomachic.*

M. How is the *French ch* founded?

S. The *French* found *ch* like *ſh*; and we retain that Sound in many Words immediately receiv'd from them, as, *Chevalier* (Shevaleér) *Machine* (Maſheén) *Mareſchal* (Marſhál) *Capuchin* (Capuſheén) *Chaiſe* (Sháize) *Champaign* (Shampáne).

M. Give another Obſervation of the Sound of *ch*.

S. Ch is pronounc'd as *qu* in *Choir* (Quire) *Choriſter* (Quiriſter).

D.

M. Give your Obſervations on the Letter *d*.

S. D is not founded in *ribband* (ribbin) *Wedneſday* (Wenſday).

M. Give your Second Obſervation upon the Letter *d*.

S. The Termination *ed* is often abbreviated into *t*; as, *burned, burnt*; *choaked, choakt*; *ripped, ript*; *laughed, laught*; *paſſed, paſt*; *toſſed, toſt.*

Note, *This Abbreviation is not to be uſed, when any Word ending in t or d takes the Termination ed after it.*

E.

M. What do you obſerve of Words ending in *en*?

I

S. Words ending in *-en* lose the Sound of *e*; as, *Garden* (Gard'n), *hasten* (hast'n) *Heaven* (Heav'n) *bitten* (bitt'n) *Token* (Tok'n).

M. What Words lose *e* in the Pronunciation?

S Words ending in *-ed* generally lose *e* in the Pronounciation, and sometimes in Writing, but it must be supplyed by an *Apostrophe*; as *scabbed*, *scabb'd*; *called*, *call'd*, *armed*, *arm'd*, *joined*, *join'd*; *grieved*, *griev'd*.

M. What other Words have an *e*, that is not founded?

S *E* is written, but not founded, in *Heart*, *Hearth*, *Dearth*.

M. What is the Meaning of *e* Final?

S. *E Final*, or *e Servile*, is that which, being at the End of Words, serves only to *lengthen* the Sound of the last *Syllable*, but does not increase the Number of Syllables.

M Give some *Examples* of it.

S. *Câne*, *bláme*, *blasphíme*, *admíre*, *demíse*.

M. Is *e* at the End, of this Quality in all Syllables?

S. No; for I have Five Exceptions.

M Give the *First*.

S. Monosyllables, as, *the*, *she*, must retain their full Sound, because they have no other Vowel.

M. Give the *Second* Exception.

S. *E Final* does not lengthen the Syllable after *two Consonants*, as, *bădge*, *wĕdge*, *hĭnge*, *revĕnge*, *dischărge*, *convĕrse*, *&c* except *grânge*, *strânge*, *chânge*, *rânge*, *wâste*, *hâste*, *pâste*, *tâste*, *bâthe*, *swâthe*.

Also *bînd*, *fînd*, *hînd*, *kînd*, *mînd*, *rînd*, *w'nd*, are all founded long, though *e Final* be left out, which formerly used to be set after them.

M Give the *Third* Exception.

S. E Final lengthens not thefe Syllables, *one* (wŏn) *gone* (gŏn) *come* (cŏm) *fome* (fŏm).

M. Give the *Fourth* Exception.

S. E makes a diftinct Syllable in fuch foreign Words, as end in *e* originally.

M. Give fome *Hebrew* Words of this Sort.

S. Jef-fe, He-ge, Mam-re.

M Give fome *Greek* Words of the fame Sort.

S. Can-dá-ce, Ca-ta-fíro phe, Geth-fe-ma-ne, Eu-ni-ce, No-e, Phe-be, Phœ-ni-ce, Sa-ló-me, Sal-mó-ne.

M Give fome *Examples* out of *Latin.*

S. Si-mi-le, Pre-mu-ni-re, Sci-re-fá-ci-as, and the Word *Ce-le-me-ne.*

M. Give fome *foreign* Words in which *e Final* is not founded, becaufe not found in the Original.

S. E Final lengthens the Syllable only in thefe Words *Tyre, Ké-nite, Shú-na-mite,* and fuch-like Words as exprefs the *Country,* or *Quality* of a Perfon. It is *fervile* alfo in the Word *Ode,* though it be in its *Original*

M. Give the *Fifth* Exception.

S. Words ending in *-cre, -gre,* and *-tre,* do found the *e* before the *r,* and fometimes are fo written.

M. Give fome *Examples* of this Kind.

S. Acre (áker) *lucre* (lúker) *fepulchre* (fe"pulker) *fceptre* (fcepter) *maugre* (máuger) *mitre* (miter) *centre* (cénter) *luftre* (lufter)

M. What *Quality* has *e Final* after *c* and *g?*

S. E Final foftens *c* and *g;* as *Lace, Race, Spice, Age, oblige, huge.*

M. Words in *e Final* sometimes take *s* after them ; what Use is that of ?

S If Nouns in *e Final* take *s* after them, with an *Apostrophe* before it, it stands for *his*, and notes *Possession* ; as, *The Pope's Eye*, or the Eye of the Pope. If without an *Apostrophe*, it makes them of the *Plural Number* ; as, *one Pope, more Popes*

M But what Use is it of in Verbs ?

S. If Verbs, that end in *e Final*, take *s* after them, it is abbreviated from *-eth* and makes the *third Person singular* ; as, *I take, he takes*, or *taketh.*

M. Does this additional *s* increase the Number of *Syllables* or no ?

S. Words ending in *-ce*, *-ge*, *-se*, or *-ze*, are increased a Syllable by the Addition of *s*. Also Words ending in *-ch*, *-sh*, *-ss*, or *-x*, take *-es*, which makes a new Syllable.

M. Give some Examples in this Kind.

S. Nouns	*Verbs*
Grace, Graces	To *place*, he *places*
Age, Ages	To *rage*, it *rages*
Carcase, Carcases	To *rise*, the Sun *rises*.
Assize, Assizes	To *freeze*, it *freezes*
Arch, Arches	To *parch*, the Fire *parches*
Fish, Fishes	To *punish*, the Law *punishes*
Witness, Witnesses	To *oppress*, a Tyrant *oppresses*
Box, Boxes	To *box*, he *boxes* fairly.

M. Give some Examples of Words, that are not increased a Syllable by adding *s* at the End.

S. Nouns	Verbs
Hide, Hides	To *hide,* he *hides* his Face
Mite, Mites	To *quake,* he *quakes*
Lake, Lakes	To *file,* a Smith *files*
Dale, Dales	To *frame,* he *frames*
Name, Names	To *tune,* he *tunes* a Pipe
Tune, Tunes	To *gape,* he *gapes*
Rope, Ropes	To *desire,* he *desires*
Fire, Fires	To *write,* he *writes*
Fate, Fates	To *live,* he *lives*
Virtue, Virtues	To *sue,* he *sues*
Law, Laws	To *view,* he *views*
Way, Ways	To *pay,* he *pays,* &c.

M. Is not the Letter *e* sometimes founded like *ee* ?

S. E is founded like *ee* in *he, me, we* (formerly written *hee, mee, wee*) also in *Eve* (Eeve) *Ely* (Eely) *Peter* (Peeter) *Besom* (Beezom) *fealty* (feealty).

M. When is *e* founded like *a* ?

S. E is founded like *a* in the Word *Ghent* (Gant).

F.

M. Give your Observations of the Sound of *f.*

S. F is founded like *v,* in the Particle *of*; as, *The King of* (ov) *the Jews.* But *off,* or at a Distance, is founded with a fine *Aspiration*; as, *to keep off, to carry off*

M. Give the Second.

S. F in the making of *Plurals* is actually changed into *v*; as, *life, lives*; *staff, staves.*

G.

M. In what fort of Words is *g* written, but not founded?

S. G is not founded before *m* or *n*, if it be found in the fame *Syllable*; as, *Phlegm* (Flém) *Sign* (Sine) *deign* (dein) *Reign* (Rein) *arreign* (arain) *Sovereign* (Soverein) *Seignior* (Seinor) *gnaw* (naw) *Gnat* (Nat)

M. What do you obferve of *gl* in *foreign Words?*

S. G is not founded before *l*, in *foreign Words*, as *Seraglio* (Seráho) *Oftiglia* (Oftília).

M. When is *g* founded *hard?*

S. G is always *hard* before *a, o, u, l, r,* and at the End of Syllables, as, *Garment, gone, Gun, Glafs, grow, fing, bringing*

M. When is *g* founded *foft?*

S. G before *e, i,* and *y,* is to be founded *foft* like *je,* and *ji;* as, *Gender, Ginger, Gypfy.*

M. But there are Three *Exceptions* to this Rule; give the *Firft.*

S. All *Proper* Names in the *Bible* have *g hard* before *e* and *i,* being always fo pronounced in their Original, as, *Geba, Gethfemane, Gihon, Gilboa.*

M. Give the *Second* Exception

S. G is founded *hard* in thefe *Proper Names, Gilderland, Gibbons, Gibfon, Gilman, Gilbert, Higgins, Seager.*

M. Give the *Third* Exception.

S. D is founded *hard* in thefe following *common* Words, *geefe, geld, gelt, get, gear, gild, gimp, gird, girl, girdle, girt, gig-giggle, gills, give, gift, gewgaws, gibberifh giddy, gimblet, gittern, dagger, ftagger, fwagger, anger, hanger, linger, finger, finger, eager, meagre, augre, maugre, tyger, target, together, begin, begirt, biggin, piggin, noggin*

M How is *gh* founded in the Beginning of a Word ?

S *Gh* in the Beginning of a Word is *g hard*, though it is very rarely ufed, as, *Ghoft*

M Is not *gh* fometimes founded like *ff* ?

S. The *proper* Sound of *gh* is out of the Throat; but to take off the *Roughnefs*, it is grown cuftomary fometimes to found it like *ff*, and fometimes to *fink* it quite.

M Give fome *Examples*, wherein *gh* is founded like *ff* ?

S *Gh*, being at the *End* of thefe following Words, is founded like *ff*; *viz.* *laugh* (laff) *cough* (coff) *Gough* (Goff) *hough* (huff) *tough* (tuff) *trough* (troff) *rough* (ruff) *enough* (enuff).

M Give fome *Examples*, wherein *gh* is not founded.

S *Gh* is not founded in the following Words, nor in any other Words, but only lengthens the *Syllable*, as, *high* (hi) *mighty* (mitee) *though* (tho) *through* (throo *or* thurro) *Vaughan* (Vaun) *daughter* (dauter).

M. How found you the *Termination -burgh* ?

S. *Burgh*, in the End of feveral *proper Names* of Places, is the fame as *burrow*, for Inftance, *Edinburgh* (Edinburro) *Hamburgh* (Hamburro) *Gottenburgh* (Gottenburro).

H

M Is *h* to be founded at the *End* of Words ?

S. *H* is not founded at the *End* of Words, if it be *alone* without *t* or *c* before it, as, *ah*, *oh*, *Jehóvah*, *Meffiah*.

M. Is *h* to be founded after *r* ?

S. H is loft after *r*, as, *Rheum*, *Rhetoric*, *Catarrh*, *Rhine*, *Rhenifh*.

M. Is *h* founded in all other Words?

S. H is not founded in *Asthma, John, Thomas Thoulon*, and at the Beginning of Words *h* is only a Note of Aspiration, shewing that the Vowel following it must be pronounced strong, as, *hand, hear, hill, hour, hunt.*

I

M. When is *i* founded like *ee* ?

S. I is founded like *ee* in *oblige* [obleége] *Magazine* [Magazeén] *Machine* [Macheen] and many others.

M. What Words leave out *i* in the Pronunciation ?

S. I is not heard in *evil, Dévil, Venison, Salisbury.*

M How is *i* founded in *Proper Names* ending in *-iah ?*

S. I is founded long in *Proper Names* ending in *-iah*, as, *Jeremiah, Hezekiah*

M. How is *i* founded *before a Vowel* in other *Proper Names* ?

S I is founded short in other *Proper Names*; as, *Mi"ri-am, Ari-el, E'-li-ab.*

J.

N. B. *The tailed* j *by some Authors is called* j Consonant, *and by others* jod, *to distinguish it from the* Vowel *i, which is really quite another Letter, and differs both in* Sound *and* Shape.

But because the Hebrew Names of Letters are not at all received into our Alphabet, I take the Liberty to call it ja, as most agreeing with the other Names of our English Letters.

So then, if this Letter be always tailed, as it ought to be, and the Learner be accustomed to call it ja, there need no further Rules or Observations about it.

L.

M Is *l* ever sounded like *r*?

S *L* is sounded like *r* in the word *Colonel* (Cúrronel).

M What Words leave out *l* in the Pronunciation?

S. *L* is not sounded in the following Words, *half* (hafe) *calf* (cafe) *balk* (bauk) *calk* (cauk) *talk* (tauk) *walk* (wauk) *stalk* (stauk) *chalk* (chauk) *salmon* (fammon) *children* (chardern) *almost* (amoft) *Lincoln* (Lincon) *Briftol* (Brifto) *Holborn* (Hóburn).

M.

M. What Obfervation have you of the Letter *m*?

S. *M* founds like *n* in the Word *Accómpt* (Account)

N.

M. What Words leave out *n* in the Pronunciation?

S. *N* is not heard in the Words *kiln, limn, hymn, damn, condemn, contémn, folemn, cólumn, aútumn.*

O

M What Words *transplace* o in the Sounding?

S. *O* is *transplaced* in *iron* [iorn] *fáffron* [fafforn]

M When is *o* founded like *oo*?

S. *O* founds like *oo* in *do, dóing, move, prove.*

M. When is *o* loft in the Pronunciation?

S. *O* is *loft* in many Words ending in -*on*, as *bácon, béacon, glútton, mútton, báfon, maton, crimfon.*

M. In what other Words is it *loft*?

S *O* is *loft* in thefe Words, *Córaner* [Crowner] *feoffé* [feffe] *Nicholas* [Niclas] *carriox* [carria] *cháriot* [charit]

M. When is *o* founded like *u*?

S. O is commonly founded like *i* in *women* (wimmen) *flagon* (flaggon)

M. When is *o* founded like *u* ?

S. *O* is founded like *u* in *Conduit* (Cundit) *Attorney* (Atturney) *Pommel* (Pummel) *Constable* (Cunstable) *Monmouth* (Munmuth).

P.

M. In what Words is *p* written, and not founded ?

S. *P* is written but not founded, in *Psalm, Psalter, Psalmist, Receipt, Accompt, tempt, Attempt, Symptom, empty, Sumpter.*

M. What other Words have *p,* that is not founded ?

S. These Words have *p* written but unsounded, *exempt, contempt, redemption, assumption, presumption, consumption, sumptuous, presumptuous, contemptuously, consumptive, presumptive,* and the like

Note, *That p ought to be left out in the aforesaid Words, because it ought not to be in their Originals, which are the* Latin *Supines,* emtum, temtum, sumtum, *if you will believe the* Oxford Critics *upon the* Common Grammar

M. How is *ph* to be founded ?

S. If *ph* be together in the same Syllable, they found like *f*, as, *Elephant, Asaph.*

M If *p* and *h* come together in a Word, do they not always belong to the same Syllable ?

S. There are several Words, in which, *p* must be parted, when the Syllables are divided; as, *Shép-herd, up-hold, Chip-ham,* and other like *Compounds.*

Q.

M. How is *q* founded in Words derived from the *French* ?

S. *Q* is always followed by *u*, and in Words derived from the *French* is founded like *k*, as, *liquor* (likkor) *basket* (basket) *conquer* (conker) *masquerade* (maskerade) In some Words *qu* is founded like *w*, as, *quart*, *quell*, *quill*, *quote*.

S.

M. Has the Letter *s* always one and the *same Sound?*

S. The *proper Sound* of *s* is foft like *Hiffing*, but fometimes it is founded *hard* like *z*

M. Give your *firft Obfervation* of Words that found *s hard*

S. *S* is founded *hard* like *z* in all Words of the *Plural Number*, and in all Verbs of the third *Perfon fingular*, as, *Names, Worms*, he *hears*, fhe *reads*.

M. Give your *fecond Obfervation* of Words that have *s hard*

S. *S* is founded *hard* in Words that end in *fion*, if it follow a *Vowel* immediately, as, *evafion, d. ufion, perfuafion, circumcifion*. But after a *Confonant* it is *foft*, as, *converfion, commiffion, dimenfion*.

M. Give your *third Obfervation* of Words that have *s hard*

S. *S* is founded *hard* in all thefe Words; *raife, praife, chaife* (fhaze) *cheefe, thefe, rife, wife, nofe, hofe, bofe, pofe, rofe, difpofe, pofy, rofy, chofe, thofe, compofe, expofe, difpofe, fuppofe, impofe, ufe, clufe, mufe* (to think) *bruife, refufe, infufe, confufe, caufe, claufe, paufe* (a ftop) *applaufe, fchifm* (fizm) *bofom, wifdom, prifon, prifoner, prefent, damfel, cafement, Jerufalem*.

E

M. In what Words is *s* not founded?

S. S is not founded in *Lifle, Carlifle, Vifcount, Ifle, Ifland.*

T.

M. Has *th* always one and the fame Sound?

S. The *proper Sound* of *th* is *hard*, as in *thin, think, thrive, throng, bath, cloth, wrath.*

M. When is *th* founded *foft*?

S. Th is founded *foft*, in *thofe, thee, then, thence, this, thy, thine, they, that, thou, thus, thefe, their, fithe, tithe, blithe, bathe, fwathe, râther, fâther, fárther, fúrther, féather, wéather, leáther, neíther, óther, móther, bróther, fmóther, hîther, wîther, thîther, lothe, clothe, clóthier,* &c.

M. How is *ti* founded before a *Vowel* or *Diphthong*?

S. Ti before a *Vowel* or *Diphthong* is founded like *fi*, or *fh*, as *Grátian, Oblátion,* &c. But there are *five Exceptions.*

M. Give the *firft Exception.*

S. Ti keeps its own *natural* Sound when *s* goes immediately before it; as, *Báftion, Combuftion, celíftial.*

M. Give the *fecond Exception.*

S. Ti keeps its *natural* Sound at the *Beginning* of a Word; as, *tie, tied, Tiára.*

M. Give the *third Exception.*

S. Ti keeps its *natural* Sound in fome *Hebrew* and *Greek* Words; as *Sheáltiel, Pháltiel, Shephatiah, Cotíttia, Adramyttium,* and the like.

M. Give the *fourth Exception.*

S. Comparatives in -*er*, and *Superlatives* in -*eft*, from *Adjectives* ending in -*ty*, give *ti* its *natural* Sound; as, *mighty, mightier, mightieft.*

M. Give the *fifth Exception.*

S. Verbs ending in *-ty,* when they take the *Termination -eft,* or *-ed,* give *ti* its *natural* Sound ; as, to *empty,* thou *emptieft,* the Cup is *emptied :* Also from *pity,* we fay *pi-ti-a-ble.*

U.

M. Is the Vowel *u* founded in all Words ?

S U after *g* is not founded, but only hardens the *g* ; as, *guefs, guilty, tongue, plague, league, rogue, vogue.*

M. When is *u* founded like *i* ?

S. U is founded like *i* in *bury* [birry] *burial* [birrial] *bufy* [bizzee] *bufinefs* [biznefs.]

V.

N. B. This Letter being as different from the Vowel u, *both in Sound and Shape, as moft other Letters in the* Alphabet, *I take the Liberty to call it* vee, *rather than* vau, *becaufe that comes nearer to the other Names of our* Englifh *Letters.*

If its true Shape *be minded both in* Writing *and* Printing, *as now generally it is, there needs no other Diftinction between the Vowel* u *and the Confonant; the different* Name *and* Character *being fufficient.*

W.

M. Give your *firft Obfervation,* where the Letter *w* is written, but not founded.

S. W is written but not founded in *Anfwer, Sword, Swooning.*

M. Give your *second Observation.*

S *W* is not founded before *r* , as, *wrap,
wrath, wretch, bewráy, wrong, wreath, awry.*

M. How is *wh* founded?

S. *Wh* is never found, but in Words *purely
Englifh,* and the *h* is not founded , as, *wheel* (weel)
where (were) *when* (wen)

Y.

M. Is *y* a *Confonant,* or a *Vowel?*

S. If *y* begin the *Syllable,* it is a *Confonant* ; as,
you, yefterday.

M When is *y* a *Vowel?*

S. *Y* is feldom found as a *Vowel* but in *Diphthongs,* or at the *End* of *Words,* and then it is ufually founded like *ee,* but without the *Accent* , as,
Dórothy, Nórmandy, fórmerly, líberty.

CHAP. III.

Remarks on the Diphthongs.

Ai, and *Ay.*

M. WHat is generally the *Sound* of *ai* and *ay?*
S. *Ai* and *ay* are generally founded
like *á* in *care*; as, *fair, hair, aim, ftay, deláy.*

M Have you no *Exception?*

S. The *a* is loft in *Calais* (Callis).

M. How is this *Diphthong* pronounced in
Hebrew Words?

S. The *Diphthong ai* in *Hebrew* Words has a
proper found *of both* the *Vowels* , as *Ai, Sinai, Bebai*

M Is *ai* a *Diphthong* in all *Hebrew* Words?

S The Termination -*aim* is two *distinct Syllables*, and the *a* usually bears the *Accent*, because the *Original* is -*ajim* , as, *Ki-ri-a-thâ-im, Ra-ma-thá-im.* Except *E-phi ă-im.*

Ei, and Ey

M What is the *proper* Sound of *ei* and *ey?*

S. The proper Sound of *ei* and *ey* is heard in the Words, *eight, sleight, hey-day.*

M. But are they always so sounded?

S. In most Words *ei* and *ey* are sounded like *é* ; as, *veil, either, key, convey,* &c. except *eye, Eyles.*

M. Have you no other *Exception?*

S. Ei is sounded like *â* in *Neighbour* [Nàbor] *Heir* [Are]

M. Is *ei* always used as a *Diphthong* in *English* Words?

S. Ei is no *Diphthong* in Words *compounded* with *re*; as, *re-'-te-rate, re-im-búrse.* Nor yet in these Words, *Dé-ist, Dé-ism, Dé-i-ty, A-the-ist, A-the-ism, Po-ly-the-ism.*

Oi, and Oy.

M What is the *proper* Sound of *oi* and *oy?*

S Oi and *oy* have a *peculiar* Sound, expressible by no other *Letter,* from which they seldom or never vary ; as, *óil, óister, cónvoy*

M Does *oi* always make a *Diphthong?*

S. Oi is no *Diphthong* in Words *compounded* with *co*; as, *co-i-ti-on, co-in-cíde*

M Have you no other *Observation?*

S. Oi is no *Diphthong* in Words ending in -*ing*; as, *do-ing, go-ing*

Au, and Aw.

M. What is the *proper* Sound of *au* and *aw?*

E 3

S. *Au* and *aw* keep ufually one *proper* Sound, which is expreffed in the Words, *auftére, jackdaw.*

M. But is the *u* never loft in pronouncing?

S. The *u* is loft in *aunt* (ant) *gauge* (gage).

M. How is *au* founded in *French* Words?

S. *Au* in pure *French* Words is founded like ô; as, *Claude* (Clôde) *debauchee* (deboſheé).

M Is *au* always a *Diphthong?*

S *Au* is no *Diphthong* in fome *foreign* Words; as, *Sta-ni-flá-us, Ar-che-lâ-us, Em-má-us, Ca-per-ná-um.*

Eu, and Ew.

M. What is the *proper* Sound of *eu* and *ew?*

S. *Eu* and *ew* have their *proper united* Sound in all Words, as, *feud, few, new.*

M Is *eu* a *Diphthong* in all Words?

S *Eu* is no *Diphthong* in *Zác-che-us, Bar-ti-mé-us, A-ma dé-us,* and fuch-like.

Ou, and Ow.

M. What is the *proper* Sound of *ou* and *ow?*

S. The *proper* Sound of *ou* and *ow* is expreffed in thefe Words, *foul, loud, cow, now.*

M. Is this Sound retained in all Words?

S. In fome Words they have the Sound of *oo*; as, *Soup* (foop) *Cowper* (Cooper).

M Is not *ow* often founded like ô?

S. The *w* is loft in the Sounding of many Words, as, *know, knówledge, crow, flow.*

M. Are there not fome Words, in which *ow* has two *diftinct* Sounds?

S. Some few Words have *ow* differently founded, for the better *Diftinction* of the Senfe; as, *bow* (to bend, and *bowl* (a Globe) are founded *properly*, but *bow* (to fhoot with) and *bowl* (a

Veffel) are founded improperly, that is, they lofe the Sound of the *w*.

Note, *that any* Diphthong *has an* improper Sound, *when one of its* Vowels *is loft* in Pronouncing.

Ee.

M. What is the proper Sound of *ee?*

S. Ee is founded like the *French* ĭ; as, *fee, feek, feem.*

M. Is *ee* a Diphthong in all Words?

S. Ee is no Diphthong in *Hebrew* Words; as, *Bé-é-rites, Be-er-fhé-ba*, but *Beelzebub* (Bĕlzebub) feems to lofe one *e*.

M. Is it a Diphthong then in all other Words?

S. Ee is no Diphthong in Words compounded with *-re* or *pre*; as, *ré enter, re-e-fta-blifh, pre-e-mi-nence.*

Oo.

M. What is the *proper* Sound of *oo?*

S. Oo has its *proper* Sound expreffed in *fool, cool*, and this Sound it retains in all Words, faving that it is pronounced like ŭ in *fool, foot.*

M. Is *oo*, then, always a Diphthong?

S. Oo makes no Diphthong in Words derived from *Hebrew, Greek*, or *Latin*; as, *Bó-oz, Có-os, co-óperate.*

Ea.

M. What is the *proper* Sound of the *Diphthong ea?*

S. The *proper* and moft *ufual* Sound of *ea* is like *é*, as, in *fea, feam, appear.*

M. Is it never founded like ĕ?

S. Ea is founded like ĕ, in bĕad, brĕad, fĕarch, fĕather, wĕather, lĕather, hĕaven, lĕaven, and fome others.

M. Is *ea* always ufed as a Diphthong?

E 4

S. *Ea* is no *Diphthong* in the Words *ven-ge-ance*, *mif-cre-ant*; nor in any *Hebrew*, *Greek*, or *Latin* Words.

M Give *Examples* of some *Hebrew* Words, wherein *ea* is no *Diphthong*.

S. *Ea* is no *Diphthong* in *Gé-be-a, Ka-defh-Bár-ne-a, Kir-jath-Jé-a-rim*.

M Give some *Examples* of *Greek* Words, wherein *ea* is no *Diphthong*

S. *Ea* is not a *Diphthong* in *Ce-fa-re-a, Ge-ne-â-lo-gy, I aé-a, O-ce-an, Em-py-re-al, Thé-a-tre, Ne-â po-lis*

M. Give some *Latin* Words that have *ea* not founded as a *Diphthong*.

S *Ea* is not a *Diphthong* in *Be-á-ti-tude, ré-al, náu-fe ate, de-li-ne-ate, cre áte, cre-á-tor, cre-á-ti-on*; except *creá-ture*.

M s *ea* a *Diphthong* in all other Words?

S *Ea* is no *Diphthong* in Words *compounded* with *pre*; as, *pré-am-ble*.

Oa.

M How is *oa* usually founded?

S *Oa* is usually founded like *ó*, the *a* being neglected in the Pronunciation, as, *boat, float*.

M Is it never founded otherwise?

 Oa is founded like *au*, in *broad, abroad, great*. And it is never found at the *End* of any *Englifh* Word

M Is *oa* never used than as a *Diphthong?*

S *Oa* is no *Diphthong* in the Word *Go-a*, nor in any *Hebrew* Word, as, *Zo-an, Zo-ar, Gíl-bo a, A bi-no-am* Nor in Words *compounded* with *co*; as, *co-ed-ju-tor, co-a-li-ti-on, co-á gu-late*.

Ie

M. How is the *Diphthong ie* generally *founded?*

S If *ie* be let before a *single Consonant*, it sounds like *ee*; as, *brief, chief.* But if it be before *two Consonants*, it is sounded like ĕ, as, *Friend, friendly.*

M How is it sounded at the *End* of Words?

S If *ie* be found at the *End* of Words, the *e* is *servile*, and not sounded; as, *die.*

M. Is *ie* always used as a *Diphthong?*

S. *Ie* is no *Diphthong* in *Hebrew* Words; as, *A-bi-é-zer, E-li-é-zer.* Nor in Words ending in -*er*, as, *di-er, car-ri-er, clo-thi-er.* Nor in Words ending in -*ed*, and -*eth*, as, *di ed, ap-pli ed, cri-eth, mag-ni-fi-eth*

M. How is *ie* sounded in Words *originally Latin?*

S *Ie* being no *Latin Diphthong* is generally parted in Words *derived* from that *Language*; as, *cli-ent, ó-ri-ent, qui-et, sci ence, so-ci-e ty, trans-i-ent, pi-e-ty,* &c.

Ui.

M. How is the *Diphthong ui* sounded?

S The *Diphthong ui* is sounded like ú, the *i* being neglected, as, *Juice, Fruit, re-cruit.*

M Is it always so pronounced?

S. The *u* is lost in *cón-duit, build, guild, guilt, guise, be-guile*

M Is *ui* always to be taken for a *Diphthong?*

S. *Ui* is no *Diphthong* in many *foreign* Words; as, *Jé-su-it, gé-nu-ine, fru-i ti-on, am bi-gú-i-ty, per-spi-c i-i-ty, gra-tú-i-ty, pu-is-sant,* and the like.

Æ, and Œ

M. What is your *Observation* of *æ* and *œ?*

S. *Æ* and *œ* are no *English Diphthongs*, and yet in the best Authors *æ* is retained in *Latin Proper Names*, and *œ* in several *Greek* Words, both sounded like ê, as *Æneas, Ænia, Mecærae,*

Œcónomy, Phœnix. But they are generally neglected in *common* Words; as, *Equity, Female,
Trágedy, Cómedy;* though they come from *Æqui-
tas, Fœmina, Tragædia, Comœdia.*

C H A P. IV.

Of Spelling, or Division of Syllables.

M. WHAT is *Spelling?*
S. To *spell* is to take *Words* asunder
into *convenient* Parts, in order to shew their true
Pronunciation, and *Original Formation.*

M. What is a Syllable?
S. Every *Part* of a Word so separated, and
distinctly sounded, is a *Syllable* or *Comprehension*
of the *Sound* of a *Vowel,* or *Diphthong,* either by
itself, or with *one* or *more Consonants.*

M. In how many *Rules* may the *Doctrine* of
Spelling be contained?
S. All *Spelling,* or *Division* of *Syllables,* may be
comprehended in six *General Rules.*

R U L E I.

M. What is the *first General Rule* of *Spelling?*
S. A *Consonant* between two *Vowels* goes to
the *latter Syllable;* as, *na-ture, u-ni-ty.*

In *dividing* of *Syllables* this *Rule* must always be
observed, except in Words *formed* and *compounded,* which are to be divided by the Fifth
and Sixth *General* Rules.

RULE II

M. What is the *second General Rule* of dividing *Syllables* ?

S. Two Consonants in the *Middle* of a Word, that are proper to *begin a Word*, must always begin the *Syllable* together.

By being in the Middle *of the Word is only meant, that the* two Consonants *are neither in the* first Syllable *of the Word, nor do end the* last.

M. What *double Consonants* may begin a *Word* ?

S. These *double Consonants* may begin a *Word*; *bl, br, ch, cl, cr, dr, dw, fl, fr, gh, gl, gn, gr, kn, ph, pl, pr, rh, sc, sh, sk, sl, sm, sn, sp, sq, st, sw, th, tr, tw, wh, wr.*

Note, *That* dl *and* tl *are often used to begin Syllables, though they begin no Word, as,* kin-dle, ti-tle.

Note, *The* Latin Grammarians *make even* ct *and* pt *begin a Syllable; and the Learner might do well to divide by this* Rule, *when he leaves a* Piece *of a* Word *at the* End *of a* Line; *but we have no* Words *beginning with such* Consonants.

RULE III.

M. What is the *third Rule* for *Division of Syllables* ?

S. Two Consonants in the *Middle* of a Word, not proper to *begin* a Word, must be divided; as, *núm-ber, pop-py, huf-band.*

RULE IV.

M What is the *fourth Rule* for *Division of Syllables* ?

S If two *Vowels* come together, not making a *Diphthong*, they must be *divided*.

M What *Conjunctions* or Meetings of the *Vowels* are they that must be so *divided* ?

E 6

S. If the following *Vowels* happen together in a *Word*, they muſt be divided, *viz. Ae*, as, *Já-el, Ga-é-ta Ao*, as, *ex-tra-or-di-na-ry, La-o-di-cé-a. Eo*, as, *pi-te ous, plén-te-ous, Mí-te-or, Thé-o-ry: Ia*; as, *phi-al, vi ánd. Io*, as, *Dí-o-ces, Lí-o-nel. Iu*, as, *di-úr-nal Oe*, as, *co-er-ci-on, co-eſ-ſen ti-al· Uo, ue*, and *uo* (except after *q* and *g*) muſt likewiſe be parted, as, *ú-ſu-al, dú-el, cón-gru-ous.*

RULE V.

M. What is the *fifth Rule* for *Division* of *Syl-lables?*

S. Let Words *formed*, or *derived*, be divided according to their *Original*, or *Primitive*

M. What is the *Conſequence* of this *Rule?*

S Theſe *Terminations -ed, -en, -eſt, -eth, er, -ing, -iſh, -ous*, ought to go by themſelves in Spelling

M Give ſome *Examples.*

S. *Bóaſt-ed, Góld-en, knów-eſt, béar-eth, béar-er, wórk-ing, fóol-i, rá-ven-ous*

M Have you no *Exceptions* to this *Conſequence* of the *Rule?*

S. *Monoſyllables*, and Words *accented* upon the *laſt Syllable*, ending in a *ſingle Conſonant*, without a *Diphthong* aforegoing, double their *final Conſonant* when they take any of the *for-mative Endings*, and then it may be proper to put the *latter Conſonant* with the *Termination*; as, *blót, blót-ted, blót-teſt, blót-teth, blót-ting, blót-ter; ad mit, ad mít-ed, ad-mít-teth, ad-mít-ting; glad, glad-der, glád-deſt*

M. Give the *ſecond Exception.*

S. When Words in *E Final* take any of

thefe *Terminations, E Final* is loft, even in writing, and then a *Confonant* may be put to the
Termination; as, *wri-ite, wri-teft, wri-teth, wri-*
ter, wri-ting.

Note 1. Where cafting away the *e* would create
    any *Confufion* in the Senfe, I advife to retain it;
    as, from the *Verb finge*, I would write *finge-*
    eth, finge-ing, to diftinguifh it from *fing-eth,*
    fing-ing, which come from the Word *fing*.

Note 2. If Words in *E final* have the laft *Syllable*
    fhort, it is a much better *Guide* to the *Ear* to let
    the *Termination* go by itfelf, as, *for-give, for-*
    giv-ing, for giv-en, love, lov-er, come, com-ing.

RULE VI.

M Give the *fixth General Rule* for *Divifion* of
Syllables.

    S Let *compound Words* be divided back again
into their *primitive* Parts

    M What is the *firft Confequence* of this *Prin-*
ciple ?

    S. A *Prepofition*; as, *ad-, in-, un, fub-, per-,*
dis-, re-, pre-, muft be pronounced by itfelf, as,
ad-e-quate, in-i qui ty, un-e-qual, fub-urbs, per-
ad-ven-ture, dif-u-mle, re-pro-bate, pre-vi-ous.

    M. What is the *fecond Confequence* of the
Rule ?

    S. Beth will be the *firft Syllable* in *Beth-a-ny,*
Beth-el, Beth-a-ba-ra, Beth ef-da, &c.

    M What is the *third Confequence* of the *Rule*

    S The *Termination -ham* will go by itfelf at
the *End* of *proper Names*, as, *Chat-ham, Leuf-*
ham, Fe-verf-ham, Buck-ing-ham, Elt-ham.

Note, *Ham* in the *Saxon Language*, which is *Heim*
    in the *German*, fignifies a *Home*, or *Habitation,*

and is often used in the *Compounding of proper Names.*

M. If three *Consonants* meet in the *Middle* of a Word, how must they be *divided* ?

S. If three *Consonants* be together in the *Middle* of a Word, there are *four* Ways of *dividing* them.

M. What is the *first Way* ?

S. If they can *begin a Word,* they must also *begin* a Syllable; as, *il-lu-strate, in-struct.*

M. What *treble Consonants* may begin a *Word,* or *Syllable* ?

S. These *treble Consonants* may begin a *Word,* or *Syllable*; *phr, scr, sch, shr, spr, spl, str, thr, thw.*

M. What is the *second Way* of *dividing* Words that have three *Consonants in the Middle* ?

S. If they be proper to *end* a Word, they may all be put to the *former Syllable* , as, *latch-et.*

M. What is the *third Way* ?

S. If the *last* two be proper to *begin* a Word, or the last of all be *l,* they *begin* the *Syllable* together; as, *kin-dle, kin-dred, mon-ster, thim-ble.*

M. What is the *fourth Way* ?

S. If the *first* two of them be proper to *end* a Word, the *third* may go to the *latter Syllable* , as, *kind-ly, re-fresh-ment.*

CHAP. V.

Orthographical Observations, or Rules *to be observed in* Writing *of* English.

General Directions.

1. LET *Proper Names of Persons, Places, Ships, Rivers,* &c be always distinguished by beginning with a *Capital,* or *great Letter.*

2. It is efteemed Ornamental to begin any *Subftantive* in the Sentence with a *Capital*, if it bear fome *confiderable Strefs* of the Author's *Senfe* upon it, to make it the more *remarkable* and *confpicuous.*

It was cuftomary in Printing to begin every Subftantive *with a* Capital, *but now it is generally difcontinued, as it hinders that remarkable* Diftinction *intended by a* Capital.

3. Let the *firft* Word in every Line of *Poetry,* and of every *Epiftle, Book, Note, Bill,* &c. begin with a *Capital.*

4. After a *full Stop,* let the next *Sentence* alfo begin with a *Capital.*

5. If any notable *Saying,* or *Paffage* of an Author, be quoted in his *own Words,* it begins with a *Capital,* though it be not immediately after a *full Stop.*

6. Let not a *Capital* be written in the *Middle* of a Word among *fmall Letters.*

7. Where *Capitals* are ufed in *whole Words* and *Sentences,* fomething is expreffed *extraordinary great.* They are alfo ufed in the *Titles of Books,* for Ornament's fake.

Some particular Obfervations.

1. C muft not be put between *two Confonants;* as *think,* not *thinck,* except before *h,* as, *clinch, ftench.*

2. E *Final* fhould not be put after a *Syllable* made *long* by a *Diphthong.* It is unneceffary alfo after a *double Confonant;* as, *Inn, Add,* rather than *Inne, Adde;* yet fome *Proper Names* retain it; as, *Donne, Deale.*

3. The *Pronoun I*, and the *Interjection O*, muſt alwaꝭ be written with a *Capital.*

4. *K* ſeems to be unneceſſary in the End of Words not purely *Engliſh* , as, *Muſic, Arithme-tic, Logic, Catholic, Fabric* ; rather than *Muſick, Arithmetick, Logick, Catholick, Fabrick.*

5. No Words of above one *Syllable* end in *ll* ; as *hurtful, beautiful.* Except Words *compounded* of *Monoſyllables* ended in *ll,* and words accented on the *laſt Syllable* , as, *in-ſtáll, re-cáll, in-róll, re-péll, re-béll*

6. *Ph* is generally retained in Words that are of a *Greek Original* ; as, *Pharmacy, Prophet* , not *Farmacy, Profet*

7. *Q* is never to be uſed in a Word without *u* after it.

8. *Q* is often uſed rather than *k,* in Words coming from the *Latin* in *quus* , as, *óblique, ántique, r líque* ; from *obliquus, antiquus, réliquus.*

9. *Q* is ſometimes retained in Words, that come from the *French* ; as, *riſque, traf-fique, pac-quet* , for, *riſk, traffic, packet.*

10. The long *ſ* muſt never be uſed at the *End* of a Word, nor immediately before *f,* or after the ſhort *s*

11 *X* is often uſed inſtead of *Ct,* where it appears to have been in the *Original* , as, *Re-flex-i-on, Con nex-i-on* ; rather than, *Reflection, Connection*

12. *Y* muſt be uſed before the *Termination -ing* ; as. *mar-ry-ing, bu-ry-ing,* from *marry, bury* ; though we write, *married, buried,* from the ſame Words.

CHAP. VI.
Of Stops and Marks.

THE *Stops* are ufed to fhew what *Diftance* of *Time* muft be obferved in *Reading*. And they are fo abfolutely neceffary to *the better Underftanding* of what we *write* and *read*, that, without a ftrict *Attention* to them, all *Writing* would be *confufed*, and liable to many *Mifconftructions*.

Stops, confidered as *Intervals* in *Reading*, are but Four, *viz. Comma, Semicolon, Colon*, and *Period*, or *full Stop* and thefe bear a kind of *Mufical Proportion* of *Time* one to another: For a *Comma* ftops the Reader's Voice, while he may privately, with Deliberation, tell One, the *Semicolon*, Two; the *Colon*, Three; and the *Period*, Four.

Their Characters are thus.

Comma (,) a circular Dafh at the Foot of a Word.

Semicolon (;) a Point over the Comma.

Colon ( ) two Points

Period ( ) a fingle Point at the Foot of a Word.

But if a Queftion be afked, there is a circular Stroke upon a fhort Line put over the Period, and it is called an *Interrogation*, thus (?)

If a fudden Wondering be expreffed, then a ftrait Line is placed over the *Period*, and it is called a Note of *Admiration*, thus (!)

If one Sentence be inclofed within another, of which it is no Part, then it is put between two Half-Circles ( ) called a *Parenthefis*; and, in reading, this doth fomething lower the Tone of the Voice, as a Thing, that comes in by-the-bye, interrupting the main *Coherence* of the *Period*, and reftraining it from being taken in fo large a Senfe, as it might otherwife bear. Each Part of it is equal in time to a *Comma*.

Thefe, that follow, are the moft ufual Marks in Writing.

Accent (´) being placed over a Vowel, notes, that the Tone, or Strefs of the Voice in pronouncing, is upon that Syllable.

Apóftrophe (') a Comma at the Head of Letters, denotes fome Letter, or Letters, left out for quicker Pronunciation ; as, *I'll,* for *I will, can't,* for *cannot*; *ne'er,* for *never, pronounc'd,* for *pronounced.*

Afterifm (*) or Star, guides to fome Remark in the Margin, or at the Foot of the *Page.* Several of them fet together fignify, that there is fomething wanting, defective, or immodeft in that Paffage of the *Author.*

Breve (˘) is a crooked Mark over a Vowel, and denotes that it is founded quick, or fhort.

Caret (ˆ) is placed underneath the Line, and denotes, that fome Letter, Word, or Sentence is left out by Miftake, and muft be taken in exactly where it points.

Circumflex (ˆ) is the fame in Shape as the *Caret,* but is always placed over fome Vowel of a Word, to denote a long Syllable, as, *Eu-phrâ-tes.*

Diærefis (··) is two Points placed over two Vowels of a Word, that would otherwife make a Diphthong, and parts them into two feveral Syllables.

Hyphen (-) is a ſtrait Mark acroſs, which, being ſet at the End of a Line, denotes, that the Syllables of a Word are parted, and that the Remainder of it is at the Beginning of the next Line. It is uſed alſo to join, or compound, two Words into one; as *Ale-houſe, Inn-keeper.*

Index (☞) the Forefinger pointing, ſignifies that Paſſage to be very remarkable, againſt which it is placed.

Obeliſk (†) or Dagger, is uſed as well as the *Aſteriſm,* to refer the Reader to the Margin. In *Dictionaries* it commonly denotes a Word to be obſolete, or leſs in uſe.

Paragraph (¶) or Diviſion, comprehends ſeveral Sentences under one Head, or Subject.

Crotchets [ ] or Brackets, include Words or Sentences of the ſame Value or Signification with thoſe they are joined to, which may be uſed in their Stead.

Quotation (") or a double *Comma,* reverſed, at the Beginning of any Paſſage, ſhews that it is quoted out of an Author in his own Words.

Section (§) or Diviſion, is uſed in ſubdividing of a Chapter, or Book, into leſſer Parts, or Portions. It is likewiſe ſometimes uſed in the manner of the *Obeliſk,* as a Mark of reference to the Margin, or the bottom of the Page. Many other Marks are alſo uſed for this Purpoſe; ſuch as parallel Lines (‖), a double Obeliſk (‡) or Obeliſks formed in different Manners (‡†‡), Figures (1, 2, 3, &c.), and Letters (a, b, c, &c.)

C H A P. VII.

Of Old Englifh Print.

THE Old Englifh Print being ufed on various Occafions, it is neceffary every Perfon fhould learn to read it, and the following Sentences are inferted for that purpofe.

Be not diverted from your Duty by any idle Reflections the filly World may make upon you; for their Cenfures are not in your Power, and confequently fhould not be any Part of your Concern.

Rather avoid thofe Vices you are naturally inclined to, than aim at thofe Excellencies and Perfections which you were never made for.

Never defer that till To-morrow, which you can do To-day: Never do that by Proxy, which you can do yourfelf.

When the Idea of any Pleafure ftrikes your Imagination, make a juft Computation between the Duration of the Pleafure, and that of the Repentance fure to follow it.

Prefer folid Senfe to Wit; never ftudy to be diverting without being ufeful; let no Jeft intrude upon good Manners; nor fay any Thing that may offend Modefty.

Avoid all Sourness and Austerity of Manners: Virtue is a pleasant and agreeable Quality; and gay and civil Wisdom is always engaging.

Whatever you dislike in another Person, take Care to correct in yourself, by the gentle Reproof of a better Practice.

Hear not Ill of a Friend, nor speak any of an Enemy: Believe not all you hear, nor report all you believe.

Make yourself agreeable as much as possible to all; for there is no Person so contemptible, but that it may be in his Power to be your best Friend, or worst Enemy

Think before you speak, and consider before you promise. Take Time to deliberate and advise; but lose no Time in executing your Resolutions.

Avoid, as much as you can, the Company of all vicious Persons whatsoever; for no Vice is alone, and all are infectious

Whenever you discourse, confine yourself to such Subjects as are necessary, and express your Sense in as few Words as you can.

Be always at Leisure to do Good; never make Business an Excuse to decline the Offices of Humanity.

CHAP. VIII.

Of Abbreviations.

AN *Abbreviation* is an expeditious Way of setting down a Word by some *Letter*, or *Letters* belonging to it, which always takes after it a *Period,* or *full Point.*

Note, *It is none of my Design to treat of the* Abbreviations, *or* Marks, *peculiar to any of the Sciences; but only of such as are met with in common* Books *and* Writing, *which I have collected and placed* Alphabetically *in the following* Table.

A TABLE *of the most common Abbreviations, with their Explication.*

A.B. Artium Baccalaureus, *Bachelor of Arts.*
Abp. Archbishop
Acct. Account
A. D. Anno Domini, *in the Year of our Lord*
Adml. Admiral
Admrs. Administrators
A. M. Artium Magister, *Master of Arts;* AnteMeridiem, *Forenoon;* Anno Mundi, *in the Year of the World*

Ap. Apostle
Apr. April
Aff Affigns
Aug. August
B. A. Bachelor of Arts
Bart. Baronet
B. D. Bachelor of Divinity
Bp. Bishop
B. V. Blessed Virgin
Capt. Captain
Cent. Centum, *an Hundred*
Chap. Chapter
Co. Company
Col. Colonel

Cr. Creditor

C. S. Cuſtos Sigilli, *the Keeper of the Seal*

C. P. S. Cuſtos Privati Sigilli, *Keeper of the Privy Seal*

d. denarius, *a Penny*

D. B. Divinitatis Baccalaureus, *Bachelor of Divinity*

D D. Doctor of Divinity

Dec December

Dep. Deputy

Do. Ditto, *the ſame*

Dr. Debtor

Dukm. Dukedom

E. Eaſt

Earld. Earldom

e. g. exempli gratiâ, *as for example*

Eng. Engliſh, England

Ep Epiſtle

Eſq. Eſquire

Ev. Evangeliſt

Exrs. Executors

F S A. Fellow of the Society of Antiquaries

Feb. February

Fr. France, French

F. R. S. Fellow of the Royal Society

Gen. General

Gen^mo. Generaliſſimo

Gent. Gentleman

Goſp. Goſpel

G. R. Georgius Rex, *George the King*

Hon. Honourable

Hund. Hundred

ib. ibid. ibidem, *in the ſame place*

i. e. id eſt, *that is*

IHS. Jeſus. *The Three firſt Letters of his Name in Greek*

Jan. January

J. H. S. Jeſus Hominum Salvator, *Jeſus Saviour of Men*

Km. Kingdom

Knt. Knight

l. liber, *Book*, libræ, *Pounds*

La^p. Ladyſhip

Ld. Lord

L. D. Lady-Day

Lieu^t. Lieutenant

LL.D Legum Doctor, *Doctor of Laws*

Lp. Lordſhip

L. S. Locus Sigilli, *the Place of the Seal*

M. A. Maſter of Arts

Ma. Madam

Mar. March

Mart. Martyr

Math. Mathematics

M. B. Medicinæ Baccalaureus, *Bachelor of Phyſic*

M. D Medicinæ Doctor, *Doctor of Phyſic*

Meſſrs. Gentlemen

Mich. Michaelmas

Midſ. Midſummer

Min Miniſter

M P Member of Parliament

Mr Maſter

Mis Miſtreſs

MS. Manuſcript

MSS. Manuſcripts

Muſ. D Muſicæ Doctor, *Doctor of Muſic*

N. North

N. B. Nota bene, *Mark well*

No Number

Nov November

N. S. New Style

Obt. Obedient

Oct October

O. S. Old Style

p. per, *by*

per Cent per Centum, *by the Hundred*

Philom. Philomathes, *a Lover of Learning*, or Philo mathematicus, *a Lover of the Mathematics*

P. M Poſt Meridiem, *Afternoon*

P. S. Poſtſcript

Pſ. Pſalm

q. d quaſi dicat, *as if he ſhould ſay*

q. l quantum libet, *as much as you pleaſe*

q. ſ. quantum ſufficit, *a ſufficient Quantity*

Regr Regiſter

Regimt Regiment

Reg. Prof. Regius Profeſſor, *King's Profeſſor*

Rev Reverend

Rt. Hon. Right Honourable

S. South

s. ſolidus, *a Shilling*

Sep September

Serj. Serjeant

Servt Servant

Sp. Spain, Spaniſh

St. Saint

S T. P. Sacro-ſanctæ TheologiæProfeſſor, *Profeſſor of Divinity*

v. vide, *ſee*

viz. videlicet, *that is to ſay*

W. Weſt

Wp Worſhip

Xmas. Chriſtmas

Xt. Chriſt

Xtn. Chriſtian

&, et, *and*

&c. et cætera, *and the reſt*

Of Figures and Numeral Letters.

One	1	I	Sixty	60	LX
Two	2	II	Seventy	70	LXX
Three	3	III	Eighty	80	LXXX
Four	4	IV	Ninety	90	XC
Five	5	V	One Hundred	100	C
Six	6	VI	Two Hundred	200	CC
Seven	7	VII	Three Hundred	300	CCC
Eight	8	VIII	Four Hundred	400	CCCC
Nine	9	IX	Five Hundred	500	D
Ten	10	X	Six Hundred	600	DC
Twenty	20	XX	Seven Hundred	700	DCC
Thirty	30	XXX	Eight Hundred	800	DCCC
Forty	40	XL	Nine Hundred	900	DCCCC
Fifty	50	L	One Thousand	1000	M

The Year of our Lord, One Thousand Seven Hundred and Ninety-one, is expressed in Figures thus, 179 , and in Numeral Letters thus, MDCCXCI.

C H A P. IX.

Of the Distinction of Words.

T A B L E I.

Words, the same, or nearly alike in Sound, but different in Spelling and signification.

ABEL, a Man
Able, powerful
Accidence, a Book
Accidents, Chances
Account, Esteem
Accompt, Reckoning
Achor, a Valley
Acre, of Land
Advice, Counsel

Advise, to counsel
Ale, Malt-Liquor
Ail, to trouble
All, every one
Awl, to bore Holes
Alehoof, a Herb
Aloof, at a Distance
Alloy, of Metal
Allay, to give Ease

F

Alley, a narrow Paſſage
Ally, Confederate
Allow'd, granted
Aloud, with a Noiſe
Alter, of Sacrifice
Alter, to change
Ant, a Piſmire
Aunt, Uncle's Wife
Aray, good Order
Array, to clothe
Errand, a Meſſage
Arrant, notorious
Arras, Hangings
Harraſs, to trouble
Aſcent, going up
Aſſent, an Agreement
Aſſſance, Help
Aſſiſtants, Helpers
Augur, a Soothſayer
Auger, for Carpenters
Ax, to cut Wood
Acts, of Parliament
Babel, the Tower
Babble, to prate
Bacon, Hog's Fleſh
Baken, bak'd in an Oven
Beckon, to wink
Bail, a Surety
Bale, of Cloth or Silk
Bald, without Hair
Bawl'd, cry'd out aloud
Ball, a round Subſtance
Bawl, to cry aloud
Barbara, a Woman
Barbary, a Country
Barberry, a Fruit

Bare, naked
Bear, a Beaſt
Baſs, of Muſic
Baſe, vile
Baiz, Cloth
Bayes, Bay Trees
Be, are
Bee, with Honey
Beadle, of a Pariſh
Beetle, an Inſect
Beer, to drink
Bier, to carry the Dead
Bel, an Idol
Bell, to ring
Berry, a ſmall Fruit
Bury, to inter the Dead
Blew, did blow
Blue, a Colour
Board, a Plank
Bor'd, a Hole
Boar, a Beaſt
Boor, a Country Fellow
Bore, to make a Hole
Bold, confident
Bowl'd, caſt as a Bowl
Bolt, the Door
Boult, the Mill
Bow, to bend
Bough, a Branch
Boy, a Lad
Buoy, to bear up
Bread, to eat,
Bred, brought up
Breeches, to wear
Breaches, broken Places
Bruit, a Report

Brute, a Beast
Borough, a Corporation
Burrow, for Conies
By, near
Buy, for Money
Brews, he breweth
Bruise, to break
Brewis, Fat
Cain, the Murderer
Cane, to walk with
Calais, in *France*
Chalice, a Cup
Call, by Name
Cawl, for a Periwig
Cannon, a Gun
Canon, a Rule
Career, full Speed
Carrier, that carrieth
Ceiling, of a Room
Sealing, setting a Seal
Cellar, for Liquors
Seller, that selleth
Censer, for Incense
Censor, a Reformer
Censure, Judgment
Centaury, a Herb
Century, 100 Years
Centry, a Guard
Chair, to sit in
Chore, Job of Work
Choler, Rage
Collar, for the Neck
Chord, in Music
Cord, a small Rope
Cittern, an Instrument

Citron, Fruit
Clark, of the Parish
Clerk, a Clergyman
Clause, of a Sentence
Claws, of a Bird or Beast
Coat, a Garment
Cot, a Cottage
Comb, for the Hair
Come, remove hither
Comet, a Blazing-Star
Commit, to do
Common, public
Commune, to converse
Concur, to agree
Conquer, to overcome
Condemn, to Death
Contemn, to despise
Concert, of Music
Consort, a Wife
Course, a Race
Coarse, not fine
Council, an Assembly
Counsel, Advice
Cou'd, was able
Cud, of Cattle
Courant, a Messenger
Current, passable
Currants, Corinth's Fruit
Creek, of the Sea
Crick, in the Neck
Cousin, a Relation
Cozen, to cheat
Cymbal, an Instrument
Symbol, a Mark
Cypress, a Tree

Cyprus, an Island

Cruse, a little Veffel

Cruife, to fail by the Coaft

Cygnet, a young Swan

Signet, a Seal

Dane, of *Denmark*

Deign, to vouchfafe

Dam, to ftop

Damn, to condemn

Dear, of great Value

Deceafed, dead

Difeafed, fick

Decent, becoming

Defcent, going down

Diffent, to difagree

Deep, low in the Earth

Dieppe, a Town in *France*

Defer, to put off

Differ, to difagree

Derbe, a City in *Afia*

Derby, in *England*

Defért, Merit

Défart, a Wildernefs

Dew, from Heaven

Due, a Debt

Do, to make

Doe, a Female Deer

Dough, Pafte or Leaven

Done, acted

Don, a *Spanifh* Lord

Dun, Colour

Devices, Inventions

Devizes, in *Wiltfhire*

Deer, that doth

Door, of a Houfe

Dragon, a Beaft

Dragoon, a Soldier

Draught, of Drink

Drought, Drynefs

Ear, of the Head

E'er, ever

Year, twelve Months

Early, betimes

Yearly, every Year

Earth, of the Ground

Hearth, of the Chimney

Eafter, a Feaft

Efther, a Woman

Eat, to devour

Heat, to make hot

Eminent, famous

Imminent, over Head

Enow, in Number

Enough, in Quantity

Enter, go in

Intér, to bury

Intire, whole

Envy, Hatred

Envoy, a Meffenger

Er, the Son of *Judah*

Err, to miftake

Exercife, Labour

Exorcize, to conjure

Extant, in Being

Extént, Diftance

Fain, defirous

Feign, to diffemble

Faint, weary

Feint, a falfe March

Fair, comély

Fare, a cuſtomary Duty
Feed, to eat
Fee'd, rewarded
Fellon, a Whitlow
Felon, a Criminal
Figure, Shape
Vigour, Strength
File, of Metal
Foil, to overcome
Fillip, with the Finger
Philip, a Man's Name
Fir, Wood
Fur, of a Skin
Flour, for Bread
Flower, of the Field
Follow, to come after
Fallow, Ground untill'd
Forth, abroad
Fourth, in Number
Foul, naſty
Fowl, a Bird
Form, to ſit on
Form, a Shape
Francis, a Man
Frances, a Woman
Frays, Quarrels
Fraiſe, fry'd Meat
Gall, bitter Subſtance
Gaul, a *Frenchman*
Garden, of Herbs
Guardian, Overſeer
Genteel, graceful
Gentile, Heathen
Gentle, quiet
Geſture, Carriage

Jeſter, a merry Fellow
Gilt, with Gold
Guilt, of Sin
Glutinous, ſticking
Gluttonous, greedy
Grain, of Corn
Grane, an Iſland
Grate, for Coal
Great, large
Grater, for the Nutmeg
Greater, larger
Greave, a Boot
Grieve, to lament
Grays, a Town
Graze, to eat Graſs
Groan, to ſigh
Grown, increaſed
Grot, a Cave
Groat, four Pence
Hail, to ſalute
Hale, to draw along
Hare, in the Fields
Hair, of the Head
Harſh, cruel
Haſh, to mince Meat
Hart, a Beaſt
Heart, the Seat of Life
Haven, a Harbour
Heaven, Happineſs
Herd, of Cattle
Heard, did hear
Hard, difficult
Here, in this Place
Hear, to hearken
Hie, make haſte

High, lofty

Hoy, a Ship

Him, that Man

Hymn, a Song

Hire, Wages

Higher, more high

His, or him

Hiſs, to deride

Hoar, Froſt

Whore, a lewd Woman

Hole, hollowneſs

Whole, perfect

Ho ! lo ! to call

Hallow, to make holy

Hollow, empty

Holy, pious

Wholly, intirely

Home, Houſe

Whom? What Man?

Hoop, for a Tub

Whoop, to cry out

Hue, Colour

Hew, to cut

Hugh, a Man's Name

I, myſelf

Eye, to ſee with

Idle, lazy

Idol, an Image

I'll, I will

Ile, a Side of a Church

Iſle, an Iſland

Oil, of Olives

Imploy, Work

Imply, to ſignify

In, within

Inn, for Travellers

Incite, to ſtir up

Inſight, Knowledge

Ingenious, of quick Parts

Ingenuous, candid

Iron, a Metal

Eyorne, a Proper Name

Ketch, a Ship

Catch, to lay hold of

Kill, to murder

Kiln, for Bricks

Kind, good natur'd

Coin, at the *Mint*

Kiſs, to ſalute

Kiſh, *Saul*'s Father

Knave, diſhoneſt

Nave, of a Wheel

Knight, by Honour

Night, the Evening

Lade, the Water

Laid, plac'd

Lain, did lie

Lane, a narrow Paſſage

Latin, old *Roman*

Latten, Tin

Lattice, of a Widow

Lettice, a Woman's Name

Lettuce, a Herb

Leaſe, a Demiſe

Leaſh, three

Lees, Dregs of Wine

Leeſe, to loſe

Leper, one leprous

Leaper, that leapeth

Leſſen, to make leſs

Lesson, a Reading	*Meat,* to eat
Lest, for Fear	*Mete,* to measure
Least, smallest	*Message,* Business
Lethargy, Sleepiness	*Messuage,* a House
Liturgy, Common-Prayer	*Mews,* for Hawks
Lier, in wait	*Muse,* to meditate
Lyar, Teller of Lyes	*Mighty,* powerful
Limb, a Member	*Moiety,* Half
Lymn, to paint	*Mile,* by Measure
Line, Length	*Moil,* to labour
Loin, of Veal	*Mite,* small Money
Lo, Behold	*Might,* Strength
Low, humble	*Moat,* a Ditch
Lose, to suffer Loss	*Mote,* in the Eye
Loose, to let go	*More,* in Quantity
Lower, to let down	*Mower,* that mows
Lowr, to frown	*Moor,* barren Ground
Made, finished	*Mortar,* made of Lime
Maid, a young Woman	*Morter,* to pound in
Main, the chief Thing	*Naim,* a Place so call'd
Mane, of a Horse	*Name,* a Title
Male, the He	*Naught,* bad
Mail, Armour	*Nought,* nothing
Manner, Custom	*Nay,* not
Manor, a Lordship	*Neigh,* as a Horse
Market, for Traffick	*Nether,* lower
Mark it, mind that	*Neither,* none of the two
Marsh, watery Ground	*Nice,* curious
Mash, the Hole of a Net	*Noise,* Clamour
Martin, a Man's Name	*Nigh,* near
Marten, a Bird	*Nye,* a Man's Name
Mead, a Meadow	*Not,* denying
Mede, one of *Media*	*Knot,* to untie
Mean, of low Value	*Oar,* of a Boat
Mien, Countenance	*O'er,* over

F 4

Ore, of Metal
Of, belonging to
Off, at a Diſtance
Oh! Alas
Owe, to be indebted
Own, to acknowledge
One, in Number
Order, Rank
Ordure, Dung
Our, of us
Hour, ſixty Minutes
Palate, of the Mouth
Pallate, a little Bed
Pale, Colour
Pail, a Veſſel
Pall, a Funeral Cloth
Paul, a Man's Name
Paraſite, a Flatterer
Parricide, a Murderer
Parſon, of a Pariſh
Perſon, ſome Body
Peal, upon the Bells
Peel, the Cutſide
Pear, Fruit
Pair, a Couple
Pare, to cut off
Peter, a Man's Name
Pétre, Salt
Pick to chuſe
Pique, a Quarrel
Pint, half a Quart
Point, a Stop
Place, of Abode
Plaice, a Fiſh
Plough, the Inſtrument

Plow, to make a Furrow
Plum, the Fruit
Plumb, leaden Weight
Pole, a Stick
Poll, to cut Hair
Pore, of the Skin
Poor, beggarly
Póſy, of Flowers
Poeſy, Poetry
Pour, as Water
Power, Might
Practice, Exerciſe
Practiſe, to exerciſe
Pray, to beſeech
Prey, Booty
Preſence, being here
Preſents, Gifts
Princes, Kings Sons
Princeſs, the Daughter
Principal, chief
Principle, the firſt Rule
Profit, Advantage
Prophet, a Foretelling
Prophecy, Foretelling
Propheſy, to foretel
Quire, of Paper
Choir, of Singers
Rack, to torment
Wreck, of a Ship
Rain, Water
Reign, rule as a King
Rein, of a Bridle
Raiſe, to ſet up
Rays, Sun-Beams
Race, to run

Round Hand

a b c d e f f g h i j k l m n o p q r s t u v w x y z

A B C D E F G H I J K L M
N O P Q R S T U V W X Y Z

He that loveth pleasure shall
be a poor man he that loveth
wine and oyl shall not be rich

German Text

a b c d e f g h i j k l m n o p q r s t u v w x
A B C D E F G H I J K L M N O
P Q R S T U V W X Y Z

a b c d e f g h i j k l m n o p q r s t u v w x y z.
A B C D E F G H I J K L M N O
P Q R S T U V W X Y Z.

Speak not in the ears of
a fool for he will despise.

Raſe, to demoliſh	*Ruff,* a Sort of Neckcloth
Red, a Colour	*Roof,* Top of a Houſe
Read, did read	*Sail,* of a ſhip
Reddiſh, ſomewhat red	*Sale,* Selling
Radiſh, a Root	*Satiety,* Fulneſs
Reed, a Shrub	*Society,* Company
Read, in a Book	*Saver,* that ſaveth
Relick, a Remainder	*Savour,* a ſmell
Relict, a Widow	*Savor,* a Taſte
Rere, the back Part	*Saviour,* Jeſus Chriſt
Rear, to erect	*Scene,* of a Stage
Rhyme, Rythm, in Verſe	*Seen,* beheld
Rime, a freezing Miſt	*Seas,* great Waters
Rice, Corn	*Seize,* to lay hold of
Riſe, Advancement	*Ceaſe,* to leave off
Rie, Corn	*Sent,* order'd away
Rye, in *Suſſex*	*Scent,* a Smell
Wry, crooked	*Senior,* Elder
Ring, the Bells	*Seignior,* Grand Turk
Wring, the Hands	*Shear,* to clip
Rite, a Ceremony	*Sheer,* pure or clear
Right, juſt and true	*Shew,* to make appear
Wright, a Workman	*Shoe,* for the Foot
Write, with a Pen	*Ship,* for Sailing
Rode, did ride	*Sheep,* a Beaſt
Road, the High way	*Shoar,* a Prop
Row'd, did row	*Shore,* the Sea Coaſt
Roe, a Kind of Deer	*Shown,* did ſhow
Row, a Rank	*Shone,* did ſhine
Rome, a City	*Sign,* a Token
Room, Part of a Houſe	*Sine,* in Geometry
Rote, by Heart	*Site,* Situation
Wrote, did write	*Cite,* to ſummon
Wrought, work'd	*Sight,* Seeing
Rough, not ſmooth	*Sink,* to go down

F 5

Cinque, five
Slight, to despise
Sleight, Dexterity
Sloe, sour Fruit
Slow, tardy
Slough, a Puddle
Sole, of a Shoe
Soul, of a Man
Sole, alone
Some, a Part
Sum, the Whole
Son, a Man-Child
Sun, the Heavenly Light
Soon, quickly
Swoon, to faint
Sore, an Ulcer
Soar, mount upward
Stare, to look earnestly
Stair, a Step
Steer, a young Bullock
Steer, to guide a Ship
Stile, for Passage
Style, for Writing
Stood, did stand
Stud, an Embossment
Straight, not crooked
Strait, narrow
Succour, Help
Sucker, a young Twig
Sue, to make suit
Sew, with a Needle
Tail, the End
Tale, a Story
Tame, not wild
Thame, a Town

Tare, Weight allow'd
Tear, to rend in Pieces
Than, in Comparison
Then, at that Time
There, in that Place
Their, of them
Through, thorough
Throw, to cast
Throne, a Seat of State
Thrown, cast
Tie, to make fast
Toy, a Play-Thing
Tide, Flux of the Sea
Ty'd, made fast
Tile, for Covering
Toil, to take Pain
Time, when
Thyme, a sweet Herb
To, unto
Toe, of the Foot
Tow, to draw along
Too, likewise
Two, a Couple
Told, as a Tale
Toll'd, as a Bell
Tongs, for the Fire
Tongues, Languages
Tour, a Journey
Tower, to hang in Sight
Tower, of a Church
Tuscan, Order
Tuskin, a great Tooth
Vacation, a Recess
Vocation, a Calling
Veil, a Covering

4

Veal, Calf's Flesh	*Weigh*, to poize
Vale, a Valley	*Wey*, forty Bushels
Vain, useless	*Whey*, of Milk
Vane, to shew the Wind	*Weal*, Good
Vein, of the Blood	*Wheal*, a Pimple
Valley, a Dale	*Wheel*, of a Carriage
Value, Worth	*Weald*, of *Kent* and *Suffex*
Volley, of Shot	*Wield*, to manage
Vassal, a Slave	*Wen*, a swelling
Vessel, for Use	*When*, at what Time
Vial, or *Phiol*, a Glass	*Wet*, watery
Viol, for Music	*Whet*, to sharpen
Vice, ill Habit	*What*, which
Vise, a Screw	*Wat*, *Walter*
Voice, a Sound	*While*, in the mean Time
Ure, Use	*Wile*, a Trick
Ewer, a Bason	*Whore*, a lewd Woman
Your, of you	*Wooer*, a Suiter
Use, Practice	*Wight*, a Being
Use, to be wont	*White*, Colour
Ewes, Sheep	*Wist*, knew
Wail, to mourn	*Whist*, Silence
Whale, a Sea-Fish	*Woe*, Misery
Wale, a Mark of a Whip	*Who*, what Person
Wane, to decrease	*Wood*, of Trees
Wean, a Child	*Would*, was willing
Wait, to look for	*Yarn*, Woollen
Weight, Heaviness	*Earn*, to get
Ware, Merchandise	*Yearn*, to compassionate
Wear, to put on Cloths	*Ye*, yourselves
Were, was	*Yea*, yes
Where, at what Place	*Yew*, a Tree
Waste, to spend	*Ewe*, a Sheep
Waist, the Middle	*You*, yourself

TABLE II.

Words different in Signification by the Addition of e Final.

BAN, Curſe
Bane, Ruin
Bar, a Hindrance
Bare, naked
Bath, a waſhing-place
Bathe, to waſh
Bit, a ſmall Piece
Bite, with the Teeth
Breath, Air
Breathe, to take Air
Can, to be able
Cane, a Staff
Cap, for the Head
Cape, of a Coat
Chin, of the Face
Chine, the Back-bone
Cloth, Linen
Clothe, to cover
Cub, a Whelp
Cube, a Die
Cur, a Dog
Cure, to heal
Dam, to ſtop Water
Dame, a Lady
Demur, to delay
Demure, modeſt
Din, Noiſe
Dine, eat a Dinner
Divers, many

Diverſe, different
Fat, well-looking
Fate, Deſtiny
For, at a Diſtance
Fare, Entertainment
Fin, of a Fiſh
Fine, brave
Fir, a Tree
Fire, that burns
Flam, a Lye
Flame, of Fire
Gat, did get
Gate, a Door
Haſt, thou haſt
Haſte, Speed
Hat, for the Head
Hate, to abhor
Her, She
Here, in this Place
Hop, with one Foot
Hope, to expect
Hug, to embrace
Huge, vaſtly big
Kin, Relations
Kine, the Cows
Lad, a Boy
Lade, to take up Water
Loth, unwilling
Lothe, to diſlike

Mad, distracted
Made, done
Man, in Stature
Mane, of a Horse
Mar, to spoil
Mare, a Beast
Mat, Matthew
Mate, or Companion
Met, come together
Mete, to measure
Mop, to wash with
Mope, turn Fool
Nap, a short Sleep
Nape, of the Neck
Nod, with the Head
Node, a Knot
Not, no
Note, observe
On, upon
One, Unity
Or, either
Ore, of Metal
Pan, a Vessel
Pane, of Glass
Par, equal
Pare, to cut
Pat, seasonable
Pate, the Head
Pin, to prick with
Pine, to languish
Plat, of Ground
Plate, of Metal
Plum, Fruit
Plume, a Feather
Quit, to eaye

Quite, altogether
Rag, of Cloth
Rage, to be mad
Rat, an Animal
Rate, a Price
Rid, to deliver
Ride, on Horseback
Rim, a Border
Rime, Frost
Rip, to cut up
Ripe, full-grown
Rob, to steal
Robe, a long Garment
Rod, for the Back
Rode, did ride
Rot, to consume
Rote, by Memory
Scar, of a Wound
Scare, to affright
Scrap, a Bit
Scrape, with a Knife
Sever, to put asunder
Severe, cruel
Sham, a Falshood
Shame, Disgrace
Shin, Bone of the Leg
Shine, to look bright
Sin, against God
Sine, in Geometry
Sing, to be merry
Singe, to burn
Sir, Master
Sire, Father
Sooth, Truth
Soothe, to flatter

Sop, of Bread

Sope, to wash with

Spit, to throw out Spittle

Spite, Malice

Star, in the Sky

Stare, to gaze

Strip, to uncover

Stripe, a Blow

Them, those

Theme, a Subject

Thin, of Subitance

Thine, or thee

Trip, to go nimbly

Tripe, the Inwards of an Ox

Tub, of Water

Tube, a Pipe

Tun, in Weight

Tune, in Music

Twin, one of two

Twine, to close about

Van, the Front

Vane, a Weather-cock

Us, we

Use, common Practice

War, Hostility

Ware, Merchandise

Wast, hast been

Waste, to consume

Win, to get

Wine, to drink

COPIES *and* VERSES *for Writing Scholars.*

ALPHABET I.

Directions for Writing in single Copies.

ALL Letters even at Head and Feet must stand.
  Bear light your Pen, and keep a steady Hand.
Carefully mind to mend in ev'ry Line.
Down Strokes are black, but upward Strokes are fine.
Enlarge your Writing, if it be too small
Full in Proportion make your Letters all.
  Game not in School-Time, when you ought to write.
Hold in your Elbow; fit fair to the Light
Join all your Letters by a fine Hair-Stroke
Keep free from Blots your Piece and Writing-book.
Learn the Command of Hand by frequent Use.
Much Practice doth to Penmanship conduce
  Never deny the lower Boys Assistance
Observe from Word to Word an equal Distance.
Provide yourself of all Things necessary.
Quarrel not in the School, tho' others dare ye.
Pull your Lines strait, and make them very fine.
Set Stems of Letters fair above the Line.

The Tops above the Stems, the Tails below.
Use Pounce to Paper, if the Ink go thro'
View well your Piece, compare how much you've mended.
Wipe clean your Pen, when all your Task is ended.
Your Spelling mind Write each Word true and well.
Zealously strive your Fellows to excel.

ALPHABET II.

Of Two-line Pieces.

AS you expect that Men should deal by you,
  So deal by them, and give each Man his Due.
  Better it is to gain great Reputation,
Than heap up Wealth with Trouble and Vexation
  Constraint in all Things makes the Pleasure less:
Sweet is the Love that comes with Willingness:
  Despair of nothing, that you would attain
Unweary'd Diligence your Point will gain
  Experience best is gain'd without much Cost:
Read Men and Books, then practise what thou know'st
  Fortune may sometimes prove true Virtue's Foe,
But cannot work her utter Overthrow.
  Greatness in Virtue only's understood
None's truly great, that is not truly good.
  Honour's a God, that none but Fools adore:
The Wise have nobler Happiness in Store.
  If all Mankind would live in mutual Love,
This World would much resemble that above.
  Kingdoms, like private Persons, have their Fate;
Sometimes in high, sometimes in low Estate.
  Let each Man follow close his proper Trade,
And all Affairs will soon be better made
  Men's Fancies vary strangely, like their Faces
What one commends, another Man disgraces.
  Number itself is at a Loss to guess
Th' Endurance of our future Happiness
  Oh! that the Sons of Men would once be wise,
And learn eternal Happiness to prize!
  Pray thou to God, that he may be inclin'd
To grant thee Health of Body and of Mind
  Quarrelsome Brawling, Gaming, Fuddling shun:
Thrice happy they, that ne'er such Courses run.
  Remember, Time will come, when we must give
Account to God, how we on Earth do live.

Some Men get Riches, yet are always poor;
Some get no Riches, yet have all Things store.

They that are proud, and other Men disdain,
Do often meet with Hate and Scorn again.

Virtue is prais'd, but little practis'd by us;
So loose the Age, that few are truly pious.

What's human Life? a Day, a Race, a Span,
A Point, a Bubble, Froth So vain is Man.

Xerophilus did well in Health abide
One hundred seven Years, and then he dy'd.

Young Men, take Pains, be brisk, and I'll engage,
Your youthful Pains will Pleasure yield in Age.

Zaleucus made his Laws so strict, that those,
Who acted Whoredom, both their Eyes should lose.

ALPHABET III.

Four-line Pieces.

A Man, that doth on Riches set his Mind,
   Strives to take hold on Shadows and the Wind.
With Food and Raiment then contented be;
Ask not for Riches nor for Poverty.

Balaam desires this mortal Life to leave,
With Comforts, such as righteous Men receive:
A noble Wish! But something's understood,
To die like those, our Life must first be good.

Crazy, weak Mortal, say why dost thou fear
To leave this lower, earthly Hemisphere?
Where all Delights and Joys away do pass,
Like thy Effigies viewed in a Glass

During the Time of Life allotted me
Grant me, gracious God, Health and Liberty.
I beg no more, if more thou'rt pleas'd to give,
I will with thanks the Overplus receive.

Exonerate your Mind of worldly Cares;
Spend each Lord's Day in spiritual Affairs:
Such wretched Souls, as squander that away,
Repent it sorely at their dying Day.

Fear not their Might, who only Bodies kill,
Yet on the Soul cannot effect their Will,
But fear God, who can Soul and Body take,
And cast them both into th' infernal Lake.

Gay, dainty Flowers go swiftly to Decay,
Poor wretched Life's short Portion flies away.

Italian Hand

aabcdefffghijklllmnopqrrstuvwxyz

A B C D E F G H I J K L M
N O P Q R S T U V W X Y Z

Riches are not for ever & doth the

crown endure to every generation

Engrossing

abcdefffghijkl mnopqrrstuvwxyz

A B C D E F G H I J K L M N O
P Q R S T U V W X Y Z

abcdefghijklmnopqrſstuvwxyz &.
ABCDEFGHIJKLMN
OPQRSTUVWXYZ.

Running Hand

Fret not thy self because of evil men.
neither be thou envious
Forsake the foolish and live and go
in the way of understanding

We eat, we drink, we sleep; but lo, anon,
Old Age steals on us, never thought upon.

He that defers to learn from Day to Day
Doth on a River's Bank expecting stay,
Till that whole Stream, which stopt him, shall be gone,
Which runs, and still for ever will run on.

If you desire to worship God aright,
First in the Morning pray, and last at Night.
Crave for his Blessing on your Labours all,
And in Distress for his Assistance call

Knowledge of Things mysterious and divine
Most eminent in learned Men doth shine.
But many Truths are from us now conceal'd,
That in a future State shall be reveal'd

Lord of this lower World frail Man was made,
The Creatures all to him their Homage paid:
But when for Sin God did him once condemn,
He's neither Master of himself, nor them.

Make much of precious Time, while in your Pow'r;
Be careful well to husband ev'ry Hour:
For Time will come, when you shall sore lament
Th' unhappy Minutes that you have misspent.

No Tongue can speak, no Pen can well express,
The Punishments prepar'd for Wickedness;
The quickest Thought by no Means can conceive
What they shall suffer who ungodly live.

Observe the wicked and malicious Man,
Projecting all the Mischief that he can,
When common Policy will not prevail,
He'll rather venture Soul and all, than fail

Prithee, Tom Fool, why wilt thou meddling be
In others Business, which concerns not thee?
For while thereon thou dost extend thy Cares,
Thou dost at Home neglect thy own Affairs.

Questions may be propounded by a Fool,
That no wise Man can answer for his Soul;
But he that would converse with Men of Sense,
Must lay aside such base Impertinence.

Return the Kindnesses that you receive,
As far as your Ability gives Leave
Nothing is more unmannerly and rude,
Than that vile Temper of Ingratitude.

See, how the Lilies flourish white and fair
See, how the Ravens fed from Heaven are!

Then ne'er diſtruſt thy God for Cloth and Bread,
While Lilies flouriſh, and the Ravens fed
   The Ant againſt cold Winter wiſely hoards
Proviſion, which the Summer's Wealth affords;
Reading a ſilent Leſſon to Mankind,
That they in Diligence be not behind
   Vain Miſers ſtrive to heap up Riches ſtore,
And in the midſt of Plenty ſtill are poor
What ſenſeleſs Madneſs does their Soul bewitch,
Thus poor to live, in hope of dying rich!
   What ſignifies it, that you Learning gain,
And unto *Greek* and *Latin* both attain,
If ſtill you want true Virtue of the Mind,
The only Ornament of all Mankind?
   Xerxes ſurvey'd his mighty Hoſt with Tears,
To think they'd die within a hundred Years;
But by his own ill Management, we ſee,
They're all deſtroy'd, and dead, in leſs than three.
   You'll mend your Life To-morrow, ſtill you cry,
In what far Country does this Morrow lie?
It ſtays ſo long, 'tis fetch'd ſo far, I fear,
'Twill be both very old, and very dear.
   Zacchæus, ſhort of Stature, fain would ſee
His Saviour paſs, and climbs into a Tree.
If we by Faith would ſee this glorious King,
Our Thoughts muſt mount on Contemplation's Wing.

Of Eaſter.

THE Holy Feaſt of *Eaſter* was injoin'd,
   To bring Chriſt's Reſurrection to our Mind;
Riſe then from Sin, as he did from the Grave,
That by his Merits he your Souls may ſave.

On Whitſunday.

WHITE Robes were worn in ancient Times (they ſay)
   And gave Denomination to this Day.
But inward Purity is requir'd moſt,
To make fit Temples for the Holy Ghoſt.

Of Chriſtmas.

AT the Nativity of *Chriſt*, our Lord,
   The Angels did rejoice with one Accord,
Let *Chriſtians* imitate them here on Earth,
And keep this Feaſt with Joy and civil Mirth.

Of the Passion.

BEHOLD, ye wretched Sons of mortal Men,
 Your Saviour sweating Blood with very Pain!
Behold him seiz'd, maliciously abus'd,
And of high Crimes most slanderously accus'd,
Let these Reflections move you to repent,
Because for you these Things he underwent

Of the Ascension

THE Lord of Life from Death himself did raise,
 And frequently appear'd for forty Days,
Then from this earthly Ball he did remove
To highest Regions of the World above.
Where he provides for those that serve him best
Most blessed Mansions of eternal Rest.

Of St. Peter.

SAINT *Peter*, in a Fit of panic Fear,
 Disown'd with Oaths his Lord and Master dear.
All human Resolutions are but frail,
Where Grace omnipotent doth not prevail·
But whosoever falls thus unawares,
Must make Amends like him, with Floods of Tears.

Of Jonah.

THIS Prophet once was sent on Embassy,
 To preach Repentance to great *Nineveh*;
But being disobedient, made his Tomb
In the dismal Cavern of a Fish's Womb;
Till sore repenting at this Reprimand,
The monstrous Whale disgorg'd him safe on Land.

On Judas

PERFIDIOUS *Judas* was but Satan's Tool,
 In horrid Treason to involve his Soul.
The tempting Silver did him little Good,
Which he receiv'd in Sale for harmless Blood
For Rage, Self-Murder, black Despair and Grief,
Sunk him to Hell, from whence there's no Relief.

On Cain *and* Abel.

O Murd'ring *Cain*, accursed from the Earth,
What wicked Demon gave thy Malice Birth?
How art thou doom'd to wander here and there,
In Desperation, Discontent, and Fear!
While righteous *Abel*, free from sordid Vice,
Takes up his Crown in endless Paradise.

On Jerusalem

VIEW but her ancient and her present State,
No City e'er went through such various Fate.
Once for Magnificence and Wealth renown'd,
And oft beset with Judgments all around.
Gentiles at first, then *Jews* possess'd her Place,
Christians came next, and last the *Turkish* Race.

The Ten Commandments.

I.   ADORE no other Gods but only me.
II. Worship not God by any Thing you see.
III. Revere *Jehovah*'s Name; swear not in vain.
IV. Let Sabbaths be a Rest for Beasts and Men.
V.   Honour thy Parents, to prolong thy Days.
VI. Thou shalt not kill, nor murd'ring Quarrels raise.
VII. Adult'ry shun; in Chastity delight,
VIII Thou shalt not steal, nor take another's Right.
IX. In bearing Witness never tell a Lye.
X.   Covet not what may others damnify.

A Child's Prayer in the Morning.

BLESSED be thy holy Name, O gracious God, for the Protection I have received from thy Hand this Night past, and for thy continual Care and Preservation of me hitherto. Be pleased to continue me still under thy watchful Providence, that no Evil may befal me this Day. And grant me Grace to avoid all Temptations to Sin, that I may do nothing that is contrary to thy most holy Commandments; but that as I grow in Years, so I may grow in good Learning and Grace, to the Glory of thy heavenly Majesty, and the Salvation of my immortal Soul, through *Jesus Christ*, our only Saviour and Redeemer. *Amen.*

A Child's Prayer in the Evening.

O Lord God Almighty, who by thy provident Care haſt ſafely brought me to the Conclusion of this Day, I offer Thee the Tribute of my humbleſt Thanks and Praiſe for that, and all other thy Mercies from Time to Time conferred upon me. Be pleaſed, O gracious Father, to protect me this Night from all Harm. Pardon the Sins I have committed againſt Thee this Day, whether in Thought, Word, or Deed, and blot out all the Tranſgreſſions of my ſinful Life, through the Blood of the holy Jeſus. Indue me with thy heavenly Grace, that I may live godly, righteouſly, and ſoberly in this World. Bleſs my Parents, my Friends, my Relations, and thoſe that have the Care of my Education, that, by their prudent Means, I may daily increaſe in Learning, and good Manners, as I advance in Years, to the Glory of thy divine Majeſty, through Jeſus Chriſt our Saviour. *Amen.*

The Lord's Prayer.

OUR Father who art in Heaven, hallowed be thy Name; thy Kingdom come, thy Will be done in Earth, as it is in Heaven. give us this Day our daily Bread; forgive us our Treſpaſſes, as we forgive them that Treſpaſs againſt us; and leave us not in Temptation, but deliver us from Evil. for thine is the Kingdom, the Power, and the Glory, for ever *Amen.*

Grace before Meat.

WE beſeech Thee, holy Father, to ſanctify theſe thy Creatures to the Nouriſhment of our Bodies, and to feed our Souls with thy heavenly Grace, unto eternal Life, through Jeſus Chriſt our Lord. *Amen.*

Grace after Meat.

THANKS be to thy holy Name, O merciful Father, for this preſent Refreſhment of our Bodies, and for all thy Mercies conferred upon us, from Time to Time, through Jeſus Chriſt our Lord. *Amen.*

AN

APPENDIX, with large Additions.

To the PUBLIC.

SEVERAL of the moſt eminent Teachers being of Opinion that this excellent Book wou'd be rendered ſtill more compleat and uſeful for Schools, were the Number of Leſſons and eaſy Fables increaſed I have, therefore, added a Number of new Fables, and illuſtrated them with Cuts, and in order to make this Book as beneficial and delightful as poſſible to the younger Children, the Leſſons that are in Words of One Syllable only, are expreſſed both in Proſe and Verſe ; and to make it ſtill more engaging, the Meaſure of the Verſe is diverſſied, ſo that they may not only be fitly uſea by the leſſer Boys, to read as Leſſons, but are alſo very proper for ſuch as are able to write, to be tranſcribed as Taſks for Holidays, &c for as they conſiſt of ſmall eaſy Words both to ſpell and write, they will be leſs liable to make Miſtakes , for which Reaſon, it is hoped, the Novelty and Variety will make them approved by the Maſters, and pleaſeing to the Scholars, inaſmuch as they are compoſed in the moſt plain and eaſy Style, and therefore better accommodated to the tender Capacities of thoſe, for whoſe immediate Uſe they are deſgned, than if they were adorned with the rhetorical Ornaments of the politer Poetry, which the Compaſs of Words, ſuch Compoſitions are reſtrained to, will not admit of.

Among the other Leſſons, will be found a Collection of ſome in a ſuperior Taſte.

Additional Lessons,

Consisting of Words of One Syllable,
both in Prose and Verse.

1

IF you have done a Fault, and are beat for it, take care to do so no more; for it is a bad Sign when a Boy is whipp'd twice for the same Crime.

The same in Verse

If you a Fault have done, for which you're chid,
Take Care to mend, and do what you are bid,
For it looks ill, if twice, for the same Crime,
You're whipp d, or beat, in a small Space of Time.

2.

God is that to the Soul, which the Sun is to the World, both Light and Heat.

As the Sun's Beams the World do warm and light,
So God Men's Souls keeps safe by his great Might

We all know the State we are now in : but who knows what it shall be some Time hence?

The State we now are in we know, but who
Can tell what Want or Wealth may drive him to?

3.

Let him that thinks he now stands safe, take care lest he fall, and so get hurt.

Be not too sure, tho' safe you now do stand,
Take care and watch, lest Harm be near at Hand

I will love all Men for the Sake of God who made them, and of Christ who dy'd to save them.

My Love to all Men shall be spread and known,
'Cause God hath made, and Christ did for them groan.

4.

He that hath God for his Friend, shall have all Things that he can want, both in this World, and in the World to come.

He, whose good Deeds have here made God his Friend,
Shall feel no Want, when Time is at an End.

They that will swear will lye; and too oft
they that will lye will steal, and they that will
do all these bad Things, What is it they will
not do? So that you must take care not to swear,
lest that bring you to tell Lyes, nor to lye, lest
that bring you to take those Things that are not
your own, for which you may die with Shame
in this World, and live in Pain in the next.

> They whose loose Lips will swear, you soon will see
> As glib in Lyes, and Hands in Theft will be
> Guard wel your Lips, and do not swear nor lye,
> Lest thus made bad you steal, and for it die
> With Shame, when it will be too late to cry.

5.

As there is a Time to laugh, sport, and be
glad in, and to use the good Things we now
have; so there is a Time to mourn, grieve and
cry in, for our past Faults and the Crimes we
now do

> As we in Joy and Sport some Time may spend,
> To use those good Things God to us doth lend;
> So for past Faults we must be sad and mourn,
> And from what's bad now with a true Heart turn.

6.

This World is like the Sea, our Life is the
Ship in which we pass through it to the Grave.
Now since the Things of this World are not
born with us, nor die with us, and we must
go out of it and leave them, Why should we be
so fond of them?

> This World is like the Sea, in it we're toss'd,
> By Winds and Storms, till Life itself is lost
> What's in't we use while here we stay, till Death
> Calls for us Home, and takes from us our Breath.
> Then why should we, who find and leave them here,
> Prize them so much, and to part with them fear?

7.

The Wretch that makes Wealth his whole
Aim, ftrives Day and Night to get it, and fells
his Eafe, his Health, and his Soul to make it
more: he racks his Brains, and ftarves his Flefh
to get what he dares not ufe; and thus he goes
on till old Age brings him to his Grave, where the
Worms fcarce find Flefh to make them a Meal.

Old Gripe doth think that Blifs is made of Gold;
For this his Eafe, for this his Health, is fold:
By Day and Night the Wretch heaps up in Store
Bags ftill on Bags, and ftill wants more and more;
Till old, and weak, and quite worn out he falls
A Prize, fcarce fit for Worms, when Death him calls.

The Mafter's Advice to his Scholars.

IF well thou art, rife foon each Day;
Firft, praife thy God, then to him pray:
Then wafh thy Hands and Face both fair,
And brufh thy Clothes, and comb thy Hair;
Then come to School thus clean and neat,
And as you come, if you fhould meet
Some Boys at Play, don't wafte your Time
As they do, for it is a Crime,
But leave them, and come ftraight to School
When there, fit ftill, be not a Fool
To talk and play, but mind your Tafk,
Which, if too hard, for Help oft afk;
So fhall you with much Eafe foon Spell,
Next Read, then Write both fwift and well
And thus by Steps mount up in Skill
In Words, and the Ufe of the Quill:
But if you do not act your Part,
'Twill be too much for Skill or Art
To make you learn, and full as vain
As if you fought for Plums in Rain.
Then, pray, be wife, and fpend each Day
To learn your Book, and not in Play.

G

The Crow *and the* Jug, *in Prose.*

A Crow that was dry, sought where to quench
her Thirst, and at last found a Jug with
some Drink in it, but the Neck was so long and
straight, that she could not get her Head in, then
she thinks with herself what to do, and at last
says she, at I do but fill the Jug with Stones, the
Drink will then rise up to the Brim: So to work
she goes, and puts in Stones, till the Drink rose
up to the Top, and then she drank her fill
and so quench'd her Thirst.

The MORAL.

*Wit oft does that with Ease, which bare Strength
can't bring to pass at all.*

The same in Verse.

A Crow that was dry, took much Pains for some Drink,
   And at last found some in a Jug;
But the Neck was so straight, she was stopp'd at the Brink
   And so could none out of it lug.

Says the Crow, since 'tis thus, that your Drink I may sip,
 I'll fill ye with Stones to the Brim,
And so quench my Thirst, as it flows o'er the Tip,
 And makes all the Earth round it swim.

The MORAL,

*Thus by due Thought, that which bare Strength can't do,
With Ease is wrought—as here the Crow doth shew.*

The Boy *and* Goose *that laid* golden Eggs.

A Boy once had a Goose, that laid Eggs of Gold, Day by Day, which so puff'd him up with Pride, that, thinks he, I will not wait so long for the Wealth that is in my Goose, as she will take to lay all the Gold Eggs that are in her; but I will grow rich at once: And so he kill'd her, and ripp'd her up, but, to his great Loss, found he took the wrong Way to come at the Gold he aim'd at, for when the Goose was dead, he found only some Seed, from which more Eggs might have been bred, which for want of Life and Warmth in the Goose dy'd with her.

The MORAL.

They who are in too much Haste to be rich, oft lose the good State they are now in, and with it their Peace of Mind, Health, and Life.

The same in Verse.

A Goose for some Time laid a Boy Eggs of Gold
   Which made the Fool think if he kill'd her,
At once he should have more than all he had sold,
   And so be made rich with what fill'd her.
So puff'd with these Thoughts, straght his Goose he doth kill,
   And with Speed he rips up her Womb
But soon found to his Cost, with her Blood he did spill
   All the Eggs that from her should come.

The MORAL.

Thus they who wrong Ways take, to come at Wealth,
Oft lose their Aim, their Peace, their Time, ana Health.

who ſaw her at Woɩk, pray'd her to leave off
and try no more, for what ſhe aɩm'd at was not
to be done, though ſhe ſhould ſwell her ſelf
tɩll ſhe burſt, yet the old one would not
ceaſe; but ſtraɩns and ſwells tɩll ſhe burſt, and
ſo was kɩll'd.

The MORAL.

*It is beſt to keep the Mean both ɩn our Acts and
Aɩms, and not to ſpend our Tɩme ɩn thoſe Things,
that are too hard, and too hɩgh for us; for thoſe
who wɩll not walk in the known Road, oft loſe
themſelves ɩn the Search of new Paths.*

The ſame in Verſe.

Aɔ a Frog ſaw an Ox eat Grɪſs ɩn the Mead,
Says, I'm ſure, I'm as bɩg as you that there feed

The Crow *and the* Jug, *in Prose*

A Crow that was dry, fought where to quench her Thirst, and at laſt found a Jug with ſome Drink in it, but the Neck was ſo long and ſtraight that ſhe could not get her Head in, then ſhe thinks with herſelf what to do, and at laſt ſays ſhe, if I do but fill the Jug with Stones, the Drink will then riſe up to the Brim : So to work ſhe goes, and puts in Stones, till the Drink roſe up to the Top, and then ſhe drank her Fill and ſo quench'd her Thirſt.

The MORAL.

Wit oft does that with Eaſe, which bare Strength can't bring to paſs at all.

The ſame in Verſe.

A Crow that was dry, took much Pains for ſome Drink,
 And at laſt found ſome in a Jug ;
But the Neck was ſo ſtraight, ſhe was ſtopp'd at the Brink,
 And ſo could none out of it lug.

Says the Crow, since 'tis thus, that your Drink I may sip,
I'll fill ye with Stones to the Brim,
And so quench my Thirst, as it flows o'er the Tip,
And makes all the Earth round it swim.

The MORAL

Thus by due Thought, that which bare Strength can't do,
With Ease is wrought——as here the Crow doth shew.

The Boy and Goose *that laid* golden Eggs.

A Boy once had a Goose, that laid Eggs of Gold, Day by Day, which so puff'd him up with Pride, that, thinks he, I will not wait so long for the Wealth that is in my Goose, as she will take to lay all the Gold Eggs that are in her; but I will grow rich at once: And so he kill'd her, and ripp'd her up, but, to his great Loss, found he took the wrong Way to come at the Gold he aim'd at, for when the Goose was dead, he found only some Seed, from which more Eggs might have been bred, which for want of Life and Warmth in the Goose dy'd with her.

The MORAL.

They who are in too much Haste to be rich, oft lose the good State they are now in, and with it their Peace of Mind, Health, and Life.

The same in Verse

A Goose for some Time laid a Day Eggs of Gold
    Which made the Fool think if he kill'd her,
At once he should have more than all he had sold,
    And so be made rich with what fill'd her
So puff'd with these Thoughts, straight his Goose he doth kill,
    And with Speed he rips up her Womb
But soon found to his Cost, with her Blood he did spill
    All the Eggs that from her should come.

The MORAL.

*Thus they who wrong Ways take, to come at Wealth,
Oft lose their Aim, their Peace, their Time, and Health.*

The Frog and the Ox, in Prose.

A Frog puff'd up with Pride strove to swell her self, till 'she was as big as a fat Ox, that fed in the same Field with her ; but her Son who faw her at Woik, pray'd her to leave off and try no more, for what fhe aim'd at was not to be done, though fhe fhould fwell her felf till fhe burft, yet the old one would not ceafe; but ftrains and fwells till fhe burft, and fo was kill'd.

The MORAL.

It is beft to keep the Mean both in our Acts and Aims, and not to fpend our Time in thofe Things, that are too hard, and too high for us; for thofe who will not walk in the known Road, oft lofe themfelves in the Search of new Paths.

The fame in Verfe.

As a Frog faw an Ox eat Grafs in the Mead,
Says, I'm fure, I'm as big as you that there feed;
So fhe ftruts, and fhe ftrains, and fhe fwells her lank Sides,
And with the fond Whim her fe'f fhe much prides.
But her Son, who look'd on, and faw 'twas in vain,
Prays her to leave off, and no more at it ftrain:
And fays, my dear Mam, if you try till you burft,
You'll juft be as near, as you was at the firft:
Yet fhe would not hear, but with Might ftill went on,
Till her felf fhe quite fplit, and fo all was done.

The MORAL.

*Out of thy Sphere, ftrive not thy felf to lift;
But reft well pleas'd with that which is God's Gift.*

The Wolf *and the* Crane, *in Prose.*

A Wolf that had kill'd a Lamb, eat him with Haste, and so had a Bone stuck in his Throat, which he could by no Means get out. He prays a Crane to put her long Neck down his Throat, and with her Bill pull up the Bone that stuck by the Way, for which, he said, he would give her a great Gift: The Crane did the Work, and ask'd for her Hire; to whom the Wolf said, Be gone, and think your self well off, that I did not bite off your Head.

The MORAL.

There are some Men so bad, that they think they do well, if they do not all the Hurt they can.

The same in Verse.

A Wolf met a Lamb which with Speed, he did kill,
That his Flesh he might eat, and his blood he might swill,
But as he made Haste, a Bone stuck in his Way,
Which he to get rid of, the Crane's Help did pray:
And told her, she should have great Gifts for her Pains.
To work straight she goes, and with Tugs, and with Strains,
In her Bill she brings up the Bone from his Throat,
Then ask'd for her Pay, says the Wolf, Not a Groat;
Be glad that you live, and still keep your vile Head,
Be gone from my Sight, or I'll soon strike you dead.

The MORAL.

Some Men there are so vile, why think all's well,
If they don't Death for Life to all Men sell.

The Ass, *the* Ape, *and the* Mole, *in Prose.*

THE Ass found fault, that he had no Horns
and the Ape that she had no Tail. Hold
your Peace. says the Mole, and say no more, for
you are both bless'd with Eyes, which I am not.

The MORAL.

Moft Men think their own State the worft, but if they would but look on the Cafe of thofe near them, they would find good Caufe to praife God for what they have.

The fame in Verfe.

Says an Afs to an Ape, I want Horns on my Head;
 And I want a Tail, fays the Ape,   [Stead,
Hold your Peace, fays the Mole, fince you've Eyes in their
 To fee how ah Harms you may fcape.

The MORAL.

We're apt to think the Gifts we have but fmall,
Which makes us ftill for more and more to call
But if we'd look on thofe, that near us ftand,
We then fhould think that we have the right Hand

The Moule, *the* Frog, *and the Kite, in Profe.*

A Moule wag'd War with a Frog, they fought for the Range of the whole Fen. But tho' the Frog had more Strength, and could leap from the Moufe, yet the Moufe by Craft was too much for the Frog; for he lay hid, and fo feiz'd the Frog when fhe did not think of it: This made the Frog cry out, fhe was us'd ill, and dar'd the Moufe to a fair Fight, which the Moufe did yield to; fo both took Rufh Spears to tilt with, and while they were in clofe and fierce Fight, a Kite flew down and took them both up, and tore and eat them.

The MORAL.

Some Men are fo proud, that if they can't make all bow to them, they can't be at Eafe till they bring both Shame and Woe on themfelves.

The fame in Verfe.

As a Moufe, and a Frog, was each proud of his Might,
And fo for the Range of the Fen did oft fight,
The Moufe us'd her Wit, and feiz'd the poor Frog,
When fhe thought no one near, and bafk'd on a Log.
At this fhe cries out, dares the Moufe to the Field,
And there, by fair Fight, try which of them muft yield.
They arm, and with Wrath each ftrove hard for the Day,
Which a Kite, that was out to feek for her Prey,
Soon faw, and flies down, and ftraight feiz'd the ftout Foes,
And in her clos'd Claws fhe up with them goes,
And fo put an End to their Words, and their Blows.

The MORAL.

*Thus fome are fo much bent their Pride to pleafe,
That they a Prey are made with Speed and Eafe.*

G 5

The Old Man *that call'd for* Death.

APoor old Man, that was forc'd to go to the
Wood to fetch home Sticks, to make a Fire
to drefs his Food and warm himfelf, tir'd with
his Load, threw it off his Back, and call'd out
to Death to come and eafe him. The grim King
came arm'd with his Dart and Scythe, and afk'd
him what he call'd him for? At which the old
Man fays in a Fright, I want you to help me up
with my Load, that I may make hafte home
while it is Day, left in the Dark I fhould mifs
the Path, and fo lofe my Way, and be forc'd to
lie in the Cold all Night.

The MORAL.

We are all apt to wifh for Death, but are foon
glad to get rid of him, if we fee, or think him
near us.   I

The same in Verse.

A poor old Man went to a Wood
    To get a Bunch of Boughs,
To make a Fire to dress his Food,
    Which done, he sighs and vows,

So full of Pain, his Life was now,
    That Death would give him Ease:
At which Death came, and ask'd him how
    It was he could him please?

The old Man in a Fright says straight,
    Lift up my Load, that I
May get home e're it be too late,
    Or else here I m' he.

The MORAL.

Thus most Men call for Help from Death, but hate
To part with Life, tho' they're in a bad State.

The Child, *the* Nurse, *and the* Wolf, *in Prose.*

A Cross Child made his Nurse so mad, that to
fright him she bawl'd out, and said, that

she would give him to the Wolf, if he did not cease his Noise. At the same Time a Wolf that was on the Hunt came by and heard her, so staid at the Door in Hopes of a Meal, but in some Time the Child was still and went to Sleep, and the Nurse set her self to work to put her House and her Things to Rights. And the Wolf watch'd so long, that his Maw call'd out for Food so that he could not stay; but with Grief he left the House, and said, he had been made to hope for Food, but had not got it, nor was like to have it.

The MORAL.

Be not too apt to trust those who talk much, for they oft say those Things they can't or will not do.

The same in Verse.

As a Wolf went his Rounds, to seek for his Prey,
He pass'd by a Door, where he heard a Nurse say
To a Child that was cross, I'll call the Wolf in,
Who'll soon stop your Noise, and strip off your Skin.
The Child went to sleep, and to work went the Nurse,
And left the starv'd Wolf at his hard Fate to curse,
For the Loss of his Time—and his Prey, which was worse.

The MORAL.

*Trust not to those, who love to talk, and say
Much more than they can do, by Night or Day.*

Leſſons in Words of One and Two Syllables.

DO nothing that may juſtly give Offence to any Body by the Neglect of any Duty; ſuch, as the ſeeking your Eaſe in God's Houſe by a lazy Lolling, or Gazing about you, or a frequent Change of Poſture, but let your Geſture there be modeſt, grave, and decent: In your Diſcourſe uſe neither the Name of God, or the Devil, vainly, nor often : In your common Life, let Virtue and Reaſon govern all your Thoughts, Words, and Deeds.

The truly Good and Great.

THey're only Great, whom no baſe Motive rules,
  Who owe no Glory to the Breath of Fools :
Friends to true Merit, to their Country dear;
To others kind, but to themſelves ſevere .
Quiet in ſuffering, with their Lot content ;
And careful to improve the Talents lent:
Good without Pride; tho' humble, yet not mean :
In Danger fearleſs, and in Death ſerene.

A Child is Man in a ſmall Letter, yet the beſt Copy of *Adam* before he taſted the Apple: He is Nature's Picture freſh drawn, which Time and much Handling defaces. His Soul is like white Paper without Blots, which the Cuſtoms of the World often render a blurred Note-Book. He is truly happy, becauſe he knows no Evil. Nature and his Parents both dandle him, and entice him on with a Bait of Sugar to a Draught of Wormwood. He is the good Man's Copy, and the old Man's Fate ; the one follows his Pureneſs, and the other falls into his Weakneſs.

Lessons in Words of One, Two, Three, Four, Five, Six, and Seven Syllables.

The Lion and the Cock, in Prose.

THOUGH the Lion is the bravest of all Animals, and Monarch of the Forest, yet the Crowing of a Cock will create in him the greatest Terror. One of these noble Beasts coming near a Village was alarmed by the Crowing of a Cock, who on a Tree gave Notice of approaching Day, terrified at the harsh Noise, he started back, but in his too great Haste unfortunately fell into the Snares of a Hunter.

The MORAL.

Men often, by avoiding imaginary Evils, fall into real and unexpected Dangers.

T........

Aw'd by the Voice of Character,
The Lion scours the Plain,
But in his Haste, and groundless Fear,
Was by the Hunter slain.

The MORAL.

Flying th' imaginary Foe,
We oft encounter real Woe.

The Magpye, *the* Owl, *and the* Sparrow, *in Prose.*

A Magpye, after long disturbing the Grove with his Impertinence, attempted to ridicule an Owl who sat blinking on the End of the same Branch for her Silence, as not having the Sense to find Matter of Discourse. The Owl replied, and ridiculed in her Turn the other's sense-

152 *APPENDIX.*

less Chatter: But as Disputes prove nothing, they jointly agreed to refer the Matter to a Sparrow, who had heard the Arguments on both Sides, and she shortly gave this Determination: " He " who says nothing, though ignorant, may con- " ceal his Folly , and he who talks continually, " though wise, must sometimes utter Nonsense."

The MORAL.

It is better to say nothing, than nothing to the Purpose.

The same in Verse.

The Owl and Magpye held a sage Dispute,
(One, Foe to Talking, t'other seldom mute)
If solemn Silence, or a chatt'ring Din,
Proclaim the best Capacity within;
At length the Sparrow Umpire is declar'd ,
She heard, and gave this sensible Award :
" Since Wit must often Intermission feel,
" And silent Fools their Ignorance conceal,
" If I conclude (with inoffensive Aim)
" Your Judgment, Wit, and Eloquence the same,
" The Owl by Silence makes securely known,
" The greater Share of Prudence is her own."

The MORAL.

Better to Silence ever to submit,
Than talk to shew our Folly for our Wit.

The Horse *and the* Man, *in* Prose.

A Horse, who in the happy Enjoyment of his native Liberty strayed at Pleasure through the Forest, had long defeated every Endeavour of Man to deprive him of his Freedom, till at last his Adversary thought of a Stratagem which proved successful At a Time when the Earth was covered with Snow, a Sieve of Corn proved too delicious a Bribe to be refused; running with Eagerness to the offered Food, the unsuspecting Steed was taken, led to a Stable, and spent the Remainder of his Days in miserable Servitude.

The MORAL.

How often do Men, for the present Gratification of a darling Passion, expose themselves to a long Train of future Miseries!

The same in Verse.

A Horse, with native Freedom bleft,
  Across the Defart ftray'd,
Nor could the Wiles of Man moleft,
  Till Appetite betray'd
But in a haplefs Winter's Morn,
  To open Danger blind,
The Steed, for tempting Sieve of Corn,
  His Happinefs refign'd.

The MORAL.

Thus Men, a momentary Joy to gain,
Expose themselves to Misery and Pain.

The old Hound *and* his Mafter, *in Profe.*

A Hound, through mere Weaknefs, Want of
Teeth, and old Age, could not hold a
Hare which he had caught, for which his Mafter feverely beating him, the poor Animal lifted
up his Head, and thus fpoke, Ungrateful Mortal, thus cruelly to chaftife me for the Fault of

Age, when all my youthful Years have been
spent in thy Service, and for thy Diversion.

The MORAL.

*Men for one Fault too often forget former Bene-
fits.*

The same in Verse.

An aged Hound severely beat,
  For Age and Weakness Fault,
Thus at his cruel Maker's Feet
  Exprefs'd his Pain and Thought
" Hard! that my youthful Faith has met
  " No grateful, juft Regard,
" Thus you my Services forget,
  " And this their fole Reward."

The MORAL.

*Mankind, ungrateful, often lofe the Senfe
Of former Favours on a flight Offence.*

The Oftrich and the Peacock, *in Profe.*

THE Oftrich glorying in her Strength of
Body, and the Plainnefs of her Manners,

thus addreffed the Peacock; " Gaudy Bird, art thou not afhamed to fpend thy Days in Eafe and Luxury ? this Farm Yard is the utmoft Bound of thy narrow Wifhes, nor can thy Soul take any Pleafure, but in the flavifh Care of thy Brood, or Contemplation of thy gaudy Feathers Learn to copy from me; my Soul difdains all Pleafure, I contemn the Huntfman, and delight in Danger, I rove the Defart in happy Freedom, equally rough in Form and Mind." " Miftaken Bird (rep'ied the Peacock) thou glorieft in thy Shame; that Difregard of thy Young and Biu- tality of Difpofition is thy greateft Infamy; but be affured, however hardened Vice may laugh at the focial Paffions, they exalt, not degrade, the nobleft Soul."

The MORAL.

A virtuous Tendernefs of Soul is far from blame-
able, and is confiftent with the moft noble Sentiments.

The fame in Verfe.

An Oftrich did with empty Pride extol
Her Courage, Strength, and Roughnefs of her Soul;
Condemn'd the Peacock for her narrow Mind,
Softnefs of Soul, and Sentiment confin'd
    Vain Bird ! (the Peacock faid) forbear to blame
" My greateft Praife, nor glory in thy Shame,
" For know, the Sentiments which you defpife,
" Exalt the Soul, and lift her to the Skies."

The MORAL.

Strive not the fofter Paffions to controul,
They blefs at once, and ornament the Soul.

Of the Seven Wonders *of the* World.

THE moft authentick Accounts and noted Hiftorians among the Ancients fpeak with the greateft Applaufe of the Seven Things, or Places following, as being by them efteemed the moft famous, either for the Vaftnefs of their Fabric, or Curiofity of their Workmanfhip:

1. The Pyramids of *Egypt*, fuppofed to be built by the Children of *Ifrael* while in Bondage for the Sepulchres of the Kings of *Egypt*.

2. The Tower of *Pharos*, built by *Ptolemy* King of *Egypt*.

3 The Walls round the City of *Babylon*, built, as fome fuppofe, by *Semiramis*, or, as others fay, by *Nebuchadnezzar*, with large Bricks cemented with Bitumen, eighty-feven Feet thick, three hundred and fifty Feet high, and fixty Miles in Circumference.

4. The Temple of *Diana* at *Ephefus*, which was beautified with one hundred and twenty-feven Pillars of the moft curious *Parian* Marble.

5. The Tomb of *Maujolevs*, King of *Caria*, built for him by h s Queen *Artemisia*.

6. The *Coloſſus* of *Rhodes*, which was the Image of *Apollo*, caſt in Braſs, ſo large, that the Legs ſtood on the Shore, on each Side the River that went up to the City, and ſo high, that Ships paſſed with full Sails between its Legs; it was the Workmanſhip of *Chares*, the Diſciple of *Lyſippus*, who ſpent twelve Years in making it: After it had ſtood, one thouſand three hundred and ſixty Years, it was thrown down by an Earth quake , it was one hundred and twenty-ſix Feet high, and every Way ſo large, that few People could fathom its Thumb. When the *Saracens* took the Iſland, the Statue was found lying along the Ground, which they ſold to a Jew, who broke it to Pieces, and loaded nine hundred Camels with the Braſs.

7. According to ſome; the Palace of *Cyrus* which was ſaid to be cemented with Gold , but others ſay, that the Amphitheatre of *Veſpaſian* at *Rome* far excelled it.

THE
UNIVERSAL PRAYER.

Father of All! in ev'ry Age,
    In ev'ry Clime ador'd,
By Saint, by Savage, and by Sage,
    Jehovah, Jove, or Lord!

Thou Great First Cause, least understood
    Who all my sense confin'd
To know but this, that Thou art Good,
    And that myself am blind,

Yet gave me, in this dark Estate,
    To see the Good from Ill,
And binding Nature fast in Fate,
    Left free the Human Will.

What Conscience dictates to be done,
    Or warns me not to do,
This, teach me more than Hell to shun,
    That, more than Heav'n pursue.

What Blessings thy free Bounty gives,
    Let me not cast away;
For God is paid when Man receives,
    T'enjoy is to obey.

Yet not to Earth's contracted Span,
    Thy Goodness let me bound,
Or think Thee Lord alone of Man,
    When thousand Worlds are round.

Let not this weak, unknowing hand
    Presume thy bolts to throw,
And deal damnation round the land,
    On each I judge thy Foe.

If I am right, thy grace impart,
   Still in the right to ſtay .
If I am wrong, oh teach my heart
   To find that better way

Save me alike from fooliſh Pride,
   Or impious Diſcontent,
At ought thy Wiſdom has deny'd,
   Or aught thy Goodneſs lent.

Teach me to feel another's Woe,
   To hide the Fault I ſee ,
That Mercy I to others ſhow,
   That Mercy ſhow to me.

Mean tho' I am, not wholly ſo,
   Since quick'ned by thy Breath,
O lead me whereſoe er I go,
   Thro' this day's Life or Death.

This day, be Bread and Peace my Lot :
   All elſe beneath the Sun,
Thou know'ſt if beſt beſtow'd or not,
   And let thy Will be done.

To Thee, whoſe Temple is all Space,
   Whoſe Altar, Earth, Sea, Skies !
One Chorus let all Being raiſe !
   All Nature's Incenſe riſe !

F I N I S.

CPSIA information can be obtained at www.ICGtesting.com
Printed in the USA
LVOW03s1932250315

431996LV00011B/271/P

9 781140 742364